Inn on the Twenty

COOKBOOK

Anna Olson

M. Olson

Inn on the Twenty
COOKBOOK

ANNA AND MICHAEL OLSON

FOREWORD BY JAMES CHATTO
PHOTOGRAPHY BY MICHAEL MAHOVLICH

WHITECAP BOOKS

VANCOUVER/TORONTO/NEW YORK

Edited by Alison Maclean
Proofread by Elizabeth McLean
Design by Tanya Lloyd/Spotlight Designs

Printed and bound in Canada.

Canadian Cataloguing in Publication Data

Olson, Anna, 1968–
  Inn on the Twenty cookbook

  Includes index.
  ISBN 1-55285-007-2

  1. Inn on the Twenty. 2. Cookery, Canadian--Ontario style. I.
Olson, Michael, 1964– II. Mahovlich, Michael. III. Title.
TX945.5.I56O47 2000   641.5'09713'38   C00-910778-9

The publisher acknowledges the support of the Canada Council and the
Cultural Services Branch of the Government of British Columbia in making
this publication possible. We acknowledge the financial support of the
Government of Canada through the Book Publishing Industry Development
Program for our publishing activities.

Dedication

To the memory of Max and Mae Olson
    53 years of marriage,
    7 children,
    19 grandchildren
    —a wonderful life

Acknowledgments

We would like to acknowledge the support of:
- the staff of Inn on the Twenty, Vintner's Inn and Cave Spring Cellars;
- family and friends who tested recipes;
- mothers, fathers, grandparents and others who inspire young people to cook;
- farmers across the country who work the land in a way that respects nature.

FOREWORD

Breakfast at Inn on the Twenty. An oasis of calm after last night's full house. Mozart is in the air, and the aroma of coffee. Across the room, someone is posing flats of bushy green herbs and boxes of perfect peppers on a grey marble balustrade. Beyond the tall windows, sunlight shimmers on treetops, catching its reflection in the waters of the creek far below. Inn on the Twenty was the first of Niagara's serious wine country restaurants, the peninsula pioneer. In Chef Michael Olson's hands, the produce of local farms and market gardens found new expression—simple, sophisticated, seasonal—a way of thinking that has since inspired the cuisine of the whole region.

It was Elvis Presley who first introduced me to Michael. I was researching a hard-hitting magazine article about the sudden proliferation of Elvis busts in Ontario restaurants. An anonymous tipoff had led me to Navy Blues, a pub-turned-eatery on an Oakville side street. I saw the King as I pulled into the car park— and he was there on the menu, too, as an item called Elvis's Whereabouts. The chef came out, a big, muscular man with a beaming smile. "It's our lunchtime special sandwich," he explained. "We call it Elvis's Whereabouts because it changes daily." I never tasted the sandwich, but I stayed for dinner—a warm salad of succulent baby cuttlefish tossed with butter, parsley and lemon juice; and an unexpectedly delicious grilled lamb tenderloin— and I've been a fan ever since.

In a business that often takes itself far too seriously, Michael Olson's warmth and sense of humor are as refreshing as his renowned culinary talents, and food writers have learned to take advantage of both. After we found our way down to Inn on the Twenty and as we began to understand the importance of what was happening there, we hit on him for interviews, photo shoots and recipes. They were always willingly given and, more importantly, the recipes worked like a dream when attempted at home without the aid of the equipment, personnel and professional expertise of a restaurant kitchen. Created to showcase the bounty of Niagara's farmland, they were as clean and lucid as the flavors on Michael's plates.

This book gathers those recipes together and marries them with fascinating little sidebars—a mosaic of lore, serving tips, wine matches and (inevitably) jokes. With Anna Olson's selection of delectable desserts, it reflects the Inn on the Twenty experience in its entirety, and as such becomes an expression of the evolving phenomenon of Niagara wine country cuisine, the taste of where it all began.

JAMES CHATTO

CONTENTS

INTRODUCTION

IN THE BEGINNING...

In March 1993, I was living in Ottawa when I ran into an old friend, Tom Pennachietti of Cave Spring Cellars, at a fundraiser for the local food bank. I knew Tom from working the Toronto restaurant scene and had kept in touch by luck and chance, bumping into him at tastings and charity events. I also knew Angelo Pavan, Helen Young and Len Pennachetti from the first "Feast of Fields" showcase, which was the start of a good food movement in Toronto, geared to linking farmers with chefs. I was surprised to hear from Tom that Cave Spring was opening a "little café" and I expressed pleasure and good wishes, mentioning to him that it would be great to work in Wine Country. Two days later I received a call from Len, the president of the winery, suggesting that I come to take a look and consider working in Niagara. I admitted to him that I knew virtually nothing of the area and had only visited the Niagara region a couple of times. I had the basic "tourist" impression, which was to race along the QEW, snap a photo of the Falls, buy an Elvis souvenir and leave town before the parking meter ran out.

Nonetheless, I decided to take a look because the whole idea intrigued me. Arriving in Jordan, I somehow felt at home and saw the potential in the concept of opening a restaurant that was very much in the country, but also surrounded by a hungry population of city dwellers. (Toronto, Buffalo and Hamilton are within an hour's drive.) The village was bordered by acres of farms producing grapes, cherries, peaches, chicken, quail, trout, tomatoes, lettuce and herbs, and that was just what I noticed on a brief tour. I knew immediately that this was the place for me.

Len and Helen spoke of their vision and it was clear to me that what they wished to do was open a decent place with food that capitalized on local produce, showed up on the plate as something that could be identified as "Niagara" cuisine and, most importantly, went with the great wines of Cave Spring Cellars.

Mark Hand and I worked the stoves the first season with a handful of local cooks, and we hoped to entertain 50 customers on a good day. We wrote menus that came from an inventory of the neighborhood's goods. I drove around, knocked on doors, and even "foraged" by bicycle for the first while, and at times felt like I was discovering wood in a forest that no one had noticed. Bob's Greens, Joe Speck's Quail, Shorthills' Trout and Andy's Peppers started appearing as nightly features. As I developed a relationship with producers, it turned into a network; over a cup of coffee, Farmer X would tell me of Farmer Y who had yellow tomatoes. Did I want any? The restaurant business soared and

we kept ordering more food. Soon enough, the tomatoes and vegetables never saw storage; we would receive them and go to work, turning them into soup or salads or preparing them for daily vegetable accompaniments. Suddenly a good day meant 220 customers! I got a huge kick out of impressing people with fresh local product. Half a dozen years before, it seemed like zucchini had to come from southern California, and green beans from Africa in order to excite people. Now I was able to brag about the green beans being picked at 8 a.m., five minutes down the road and, by the way, the farmer's daughter is bussing your table tonight! Whether it was discovering Niagara, national pride, the emergence of Niagara wine or just wanting to know where their food came from, people were gobbling up what we were serving.

To meet business demands, we increased staff and hired a young woman named Anna who came to us after working in the United States. She worked on the line for two years and then took over as pastry chef. I always wanted to be with someone who made a lot of dough, and Anna agreed to marry me in 1999.

EVOLUTION

As the business grew, farmers began coming to me instead of the other way around. We co-operated to form a network of suppliers and chefs, which continues today under the auspices of Taste of Niagara. If a new chef moves into the area, I'm very happy to share any information or sources he or she may require.

Some producers grow to our specifications and I meet with others in the winter with a seed catalogue to determine the next summer's crop. In soil that once grew tomatoes and squash, Dave Irish now presides over meticulously maintained rows of striped beets, okra, jalapeños, Swiss chard, Thai basil, purple cauliflower, cobless corn and eggplant in a variety of colors and shapes. When a fruit or vegetable comes into its own during that fifteen seconds of fame called "in season," the farmers appear at the back door of the restaurant like proud family with baby photos. A cook living in the country has an easier time developing chef-farmer connections than our city cousins do, simply because of proximity.

THE VINTNER'S INN

Customers coming to the restaurant from outside our area would call to book a table and quite often ask for advice on a place to stay. The message was consistent: they wanted a country inn with beautiful rooms, luxurious bathrooms, antiques, fireplaces and so on. At this point, Len and Helen started to hear a voice saying, "If you build it, they will come."

Len negotiated the purchase of the building across the street and Helen went to work creating an environment of country sophistication that provided a calm retreat for any traveler.

Having overnight guests meant serving breakfast at Inn on the Twenty. This lengthened the work day for the kitchen and dining room staff so that we currently operate 20 out of 24 hours each day. Along with couples on romantic retreats, the Vintner's Inn became attractive to business clients who wanted a quiet spot for small conferences. The Inn has a boardroom for them, and easy access to tours, golf, cycling, great wine, and some pretty good food. The village of Jordan has many shops featuring antiques, art, clothing, design and gardening.

All that was missing was the means to cater to large groups.

THE PRIVATE DINING ROOMS

The second floor of Inn on the Twenty had been an empty shell used for storage until the start of 1999. Blueprints rolled out, the trades arrived and work started on the Jordan Room and Windows on the Twenty, totalling 200 new seats. We outfitted a second kitchen and built a stand-alone bakeshop.

Finally, we could accommodate weddings and other large parties, which we had turned away in the past. Now a good day means feeding 600 guests and the kitchen staff has grown to 50.

Despite our growth, our style of food has remained true to our original goal; we serve tasty dishes made from local products in a way that pairs well with wine. Many of our guests ask for recipes, which results in several hours' work weekly for Anna, so it seemed logical to gather the most popular recipes into a book.

We hope that this inspires you to visit Niagara but, more importantly, encourages you to cook with good ingredients in a simple way for people you like. I think it is great to peek out into the dining room on a busy Saturday night and see folks enjoying themselves. The best meal memories have food as a great supporting actor—it is good company that makes it all happen.

The food and wine improves in Niagara every season and there are so many talented people dedicated to their craft who enjoy working and living here. We feel lucky to have jobs that we enjoy. Life is good. You should come see us sometime.

MICHAEL AND ANNA OLSON

12

FOOD AND WINE

Choosing appropriate wine to go with dishes is a point of interest when entertaining, but should not be cause for undue stress. Is Sauvignon Blanc the wine to pair with rack of lamb? I would say absolutely not, but the second part of that answer is that the world would likely not stop spinning and life would go on if you were to serve it. The food and wine world can tend to obsess over this issue and it is a topic that could, and in some cases does, merit a life-long study. At the end of the day taste in food and wine is so subjective that the most important opinion is always that of the person whose mouth is full of them. If you really do like Sauvignon Blanc with lamb, then, by all means, enjoy.

There are several books on food and wine matching and the Internet is full of articles on the subject if one is inclined to study further. The old rules suggested that you go from driest to sweetest, and lightest to heaviest over the course of a meal; white wine goes with fish and red wine goes with meat. The rules have changed, but really not that much. Yes, tuna does go well with Merlot and pork is excellent with Riesling but, by and large, you are safe with the old rules. I would suggest that if you are experimenting with international cuisines, you should accompany the food with either wines of the same region or wines made in the style of that country. While European wines are specifically associated with growing regions, Niagara produces styles of wine that supersede geography. For example, Cave Spring produces top-notch Rieslings comparable to Germany's, Chardonnays in the style of Burgundy and Rosés in the manner of Southern France.

In a good match, the wine makes the food taste better and the food rounds out and balances the wine. The characteristics of each wine are unique and consideration must be given to how food complements or contrasts with the varieties.

NON-OAKED WHITE WINES

The two characteristics of non-oaked white wines that determine food compatibility are residual sugar and acidity. Residual sugar refers to the level of sweetness due to the sugar left in the wine after fermentation. This is a result of either a winemaking technique of stopping the fermentation or there being so much sugar in the ripe grapes that the wine will not ferment to dryness. Residual sugar tends to dictate the weight of a wine, so a completely dry white will seem lighter than one with just a little more sweetness. This can make a difference in choosing a wine compatible with clean, austere flavors like delicate seafood. Acidity tends to make the wine very much alive and helps show off the fruit; it also helps to stand up to rich, fatty foods.

A good food and wine match is one that is obviously pleasant, where the food makes the wine taste better than on its own, and vice versa. For a simple illustration of this, choose two Rieslings (such as Cave Spring Dry Riesling and Off-Dry Riesling) and taste them back-to-back with a straightforward flavor like our Pan-fried Scallops. Compare the acidity and sweetness levels and determine which suits you best.

OAK-AGED WHITE WINES

Oak aging of Chardonnay is a process by which the wine is either stored in oak barrels or fermented in them to extract flavors from the wood. These tend to show up on your palate as smoky, nutty, vanilla and even spicy flavors.

The dairy note associated with Chardonnays comes from a process that takes place in the barrel called "malo-lactic fermentation." It is a secondary fermentation that converts natural acids in the grape juice from malic acid (like apple juice) to lactic acid (like milk). This often comes across as a rich, buttery smell. Chardonnays that have gone through this process show a natural affinity to foods rich in dairy ingredients.

An easy exercise to do at home is to try a non-oaked wine and an oaky one with a piece of cheese, such as cheddar or Brie, to determine which wine you favor with the dairy. The next step is to serve the Pan Roasted Chicken with Caramelized Shallots and Sweet Potato and Celery Root Gratin and try both wines with these dishes. Who thought education could be so rewarding?

LIGHT RED WINES

Light-bodied red wines, such as Gamay, are generally meant to be consumed within a couple of years as they are fruity and slightly

14

acidic. Gamay shows off herbal characteristics and its acidity makes it compatible with tomato sauces. Try it with our Acini di Pepe with Eggplant, Tomato and Romano, or with the Grilled Summer Vegetables on Goat Cheese Fondant.

BIG REDS

Richer red wines are a little more complex as they have tannins in them, which will mellow as the wine ages. Tannins make your mouth feel dry, like tea that has been oversteeped. Cabernet Sauvignon is such a wine and tends to match very well with proteins, especially beef or lamb. The full, peppery, rich mouth-feel of a rack of lamb needs an equally rich wine to complement its flavor.

Young tannic reds do not pair well with acidic foods as they tend to amplify the dry mouth experience. Drink a Cabernet with something lemony and you may feel as though your head is about to cave in.

DESSERT WINES

Sweet wines use the grapes that have been left on the vine late into the season and, in the case of icewine, allowed to freeze rock-hard. While the grape hangs on the vine, the natural sugars concentrate as water evaporates from the fruit. Similar to the idea of reducing a stock, the grape juice becomes more concen-

trated in its flavor, sweetness and acidity. Late harvest wines are best suited to simple fruit dessert preparations, especially those that are similar to the wine characteristics, such as apricot, pear and apple.

Icewines tend to be "dessert in a glass," where they are better off left alone; something reasonably acidic or sweet may stand up, but icewine can tend to overwhelm a lot of desserts.

It is very interesting to pay attention to how food and wine affect each other and when you do find a match that you are confident works reasonably well, it can become your "signature dish."

BASICS

Cooking requires the passion of an artist and the practical approach of a scientist. The artistry can be affected by your style, mood or personality but the science of cooking does not change. Sugars will caramelize, water will turn to steam, proteins will coagulate and fermentation will occur. Arming yourself with a set of basic skills allows you to cook as well as anyone, but at your own pace.

The building block for savory cooking is always a well-made stock. Take the time to make your own, on an as-needed basis or as a weekly ritual. It really does make a difference in soups, sauces, stews, rice and vegetables. At the restaurant, we say that if a culinary student is to learn only one thing at cooking school, it should be the importance of a good chicken stock.

Light Chicken Stock

A FLAVORFUL CHICKEN STOCK can be produced from a whole chicken, chicken bones or chicken pieces. While most restaurants, ourselves included, use chicken bones for stock, chicken leg quarters make the best base stock at home. They are affordable and reduce the cooking time of your stock to only 2 hours instead of our requisite 4 to 6 hours.

Bringing the stock up to a simmer very slowly ensures that the broth will be clear and the flavor clean. While it's the most basic of culinary preparations, a good stock is the cornerstone of many dishes and is also a gratifying accomplishment in itself.

Yields 12 cups (3 L)

4 lbs.	chicken leg quarters	1.8 kg
12 cups	cold water	3 L
2	onions, peeled and roughly chopped	2
2	ribs celery, chopped	2
2	carrots, peeled and chopped	2
1	sprig fresh thyme	1
1	bay leaf	1
4	whole black peppercorns	4
2	parsley stems (optional)	2

Place chicken quarters into a medium stockpot and cover with cold water. Bring slowly to a simmer. As stock warms, residue and fat will come to the surface; using a spoon, gently skim residue off and discard. Do not stir stock.

Once stock reaches a simmer, add remaining ingredients. Continue to simmer stock, uncovered, for 2 hours, skimming regularly. The longer stock simmers, the greater flavor it will attain.

Strain off solids and reserve liquid for future use. You can use the leg meat for soups, casseroles or sandwiches. Stock freezes well.

There are convenience products available for use as stock, but many of them are made with MSG or salt, which are not necessary. Stocks can be simmered while you are doing other things, and they really make the house smell great! If you have the space, make a large batch and freeze it in plastic containers.

Dark Chicken Stock

THE RICHNESS and deep color of dark chicken stock add flavor and color to many dishes, particularly to autumn and winter foods. The time you take to roast the chicken bones is rewarded by a richer taste and an inviting aroma in the kitchen. While we recommend chicken leg quarters for your light chicken stock, you do need chicken bones in order to prepare a dark chicken stock.

Yields 12 cups (3 L)

4 lbs.	chicken bones	1.8 kg
2	onions, peeled and roughly chopped	2
2	ribs celery, chopped	2
2	carrots, peeled and chopped	2
½ cup	white wine	120 mL
12 cups	cold water	3 L
1	sprig fresh thyme	1
1	bay leaf	1
4	whole black peppercorns	4
2	parsley stems (optional)	2

Preheat oven to 375°F (190°C). Place chicken bones and vegetables in a roasting pan. Roast bones until they have taken on a deep brown color, 30 to 40 minutes. Remove bones and vegetables from pan into stockpot.

To deglaze, pour white wine into roasting pan and place pan over stove burner at medium heat. Using a wooden spoon, gently scrape residue from bottom of pan and add it to stockpot. Cover bones with cold water, add herbs and peppercorns and bring slowly to a simmer.

As stock warms, residue and fat will come to the surface; using a spoon, gently skim residue off and discard. Do not stir stock. Continue to simmer stock, uncovered, for 4 to 6 hours, skimming regularly. The longer stock simmers, the greater flavor it will attain.

Strain off solids and reserve liquid for future use. Stock freezes well.

Great restaurant sauces get their intensity from reducing stocks down to a molasses-like glaze. Remember—reducing is simply evaporating extra water, thus concentrating flavor.

Deglazing means adding a cold liquid to free up natural sugars that have caramelized onto the surface of the pan. A wooden spoon helps to scrape and break these "tasty bits" into the solution.

Dark Beef Stock

THE REDUCTION of a rich beef stock makes a great sauce for many meats, especially with the addition of such things as caramelized shallots or mushrooms. Roasting the vegetables with the beef adds to the depth of color and flavor. The inclusion of tomato in this recipe adds to the depth, but is not an essential ingredient.

Yields 8 cups (2 L)

2 lbs.	diced stewing beef	900 g
	or	
4 lbs.	beef bones	1.8 kg
2	onions, skins on, chopped	2
2	ribs celery, chopped	2
2	carrots, chopped	2
$\frac{1}{2}$ cup	red wine	120 mL
8 cups	cold water	2 L
1	tomato, chopped (optional)	1
1	sprig fresh thyme	1
1	bay leaf	1
4	black peppercorns	4
2	parsley stems	2

Preheat oven to 400°F (200°C). Place diced beef or bones and vegetables in a roasting pan. Roast bones until they have taken on a deep brown color, 30 to 40 minutes. Remove bones and vegetables from pan and place in a medium stockpot.

To deglaze, pour red wine into roasting pan and place pan over stove burner at medium heat. Using a wooden spoon, gently scrape residue from bottom of pan and add it to stockpot. Cover bones with cold water. Add tomato (if using), herbs and peppercorns and bring slowly to a simmer.

As stock warms, residue and fat will surface; using a spoon, gently skim residue off and discard. Do not stir stock. Continue to simmer stock, uncovered, for 6 hours, skimming regularly. The longer stock simmers, the greater flavor it will attain.

Strain off solids and reserve liquid for future use. Stock freezes well.

A great stock will make your lips stick together and will be turned into jelly as it is refrigerated. Don't be afraid to really brown the bones and mirepoix (the vegetable component) to bring out a richness and roundness.

Fish Stock

ASK FOR FISH BONES and trimmings at the fish department of your local grocery store. They are in abundance and usually at a reasonable cost. Do remember that the stronger the fish, the stronger the resulting flavor; therefore, if you do not favor mackerel or kingfish, do not include them in your stock.

The delicate texture of fish means that it does not require a long time to extract its flavor.

Yields 8 cups (2 L)

3 lbs.	fish bones	1.4 kg
	or	
1½ lbs.	fish trimmings	680 g
1 cup	white wine	240 mL
7 cups	water	1.75 L
2	onions, peeled and chopped	2
1	rib celery, chopped	1
1	tomato, chopped	1
1	sprig fresh thyme	1
1	bay leaf	1
4	whole black peppercorns	4
1	lemon, cut in half	1

In a medium stockpot, place fish bones or trimmings and cover with white wine and water. Bring gradually to a simmer, skimming and discarding any impurities that may rise to the surface.

Once stock is at a simmer, add vegetables, seasonings and lemon. Continue to simmer for 20 minutes. Strain off solids and reserve liquid. Cool and refrigerate or freeze until ready to use.

A "fumet," or fish stock, should have a subtle, clean flavor that won't overpower the dish in which it is used. Don't use strong herbs such as rosemary or sage when cooking delicate seafood; fine herbs like tarragon, chives, parsley or mint are better suited to these recipes.

Shellfish Stock

IF YOU PURCHASE unpeeled raw shrimp, be sure to save the shells—they're full of flavor! Simply place them in the freezer (they are quite compact) until you have enough to use. *Yields 8 cups (2 L)*

2 Tbsp.	vegetable oil	30 mL
1½ lbs.	shrimp shells	680 g
	or	
3 lbs.	lobster or crab shells	1.4 kg
1 cup	white wine	240 mL
7 cups	cold water	1.75 L
2	onions, peeled and chopped	2
1	rib celery, chopped	1
1	tomato, chopped	1
1	sprig fresh thyme	1
1	bay leaf	1
2	parsley stems	2
1	lemon, cut in half	1

In a medium stockpot, heat oil over medium heat and sauté shells until they are pink, 4 to 6 minutes. Cover with white wine and water. Bring gradually to a simmer, skimming and discarding any impurities that rise to the surface.

Once stock is at a simmer, add vegetables, seasonings and lemon. Continue to simmer for 20 minutes. Strain off solids and reserve liquid. Cool and refrigerate or freeze until ready to use.

Vegetable Stock

THIS STOCK can be substituted anywhere a vegetarian replacement needs to be made. As vegetable stock only requires an hour of simmering, it is also convenient if you do not have time to make a chicken stock.

Yields 8 cups (2 L)

Base Stock

3	onions, peeled and chopped	3
3	ribs celery, chopped	3
3	carrots, peeled and chopped	3
2	sprigs fresh thyme	2
1	bay leaf	1
4	whole black peppercorns	4
1	lemon, cut in half	1

Flavoring Options

4	ripe tomatoes, chopped	4
6	cobs corn, kernels removed	6
1 lb.	shucked pea pods	455 g
1	head roasted garlic	1
1	bunch leek tops, washed and chopped	1
2 cups	basil stems	475 mL
½ cup	rosemary stems	120 mL

Place all base stock ingredients and desired flavoring options in a medium stockpot and cover with 8 cups (2 L) cold water. Bring to a simmer and cook for 1 hour.

Drain and discard solids, while reserving liquid. Chill and refrigerate or freeze until ready to use.

Vegetable stock can be regarded as a "clean the fridge" base. In the summer, items such as corn cobs, emptied pea pods and basil stems are plentiful. Winter abounds with leek trimmings, parsnips and cleaned heads of roasted garlic. All of these items make seasonal-appropriate additions to a vegetable stock: use your imagination!

Roasted Garlic

ALTHOUGH MANY RECIPES in this book only call for a few cloves of roasted garlic, it makes sense to roast more than you need. Roasted garlic keeps well for a week in an airtight container in the fridge, or cloves puréed with a little olive oil can be frozen.

Yields 6 heads

6	heads garlic	6
3 Tbsp.	olive oil	45 mL
1½ Tbsp.	unsalted butter	22.5 mL
½ tsp.	chopped fresh thyme	2.5 mL
	salt and pepper	

Preheat oven to 350°F (175°C). Slice tops of garlic heads to expose cloves and place garlic in a baking dish. Brush tops with olive oil, dot with butter, and sprinkle with thyme, salt and pepper. Cover dish with foil. Bake for 30 minutes. Remove foil and roast until cloves are browned and tender, about 20 more minutes.

The usual sharpness of garlic is mellowed by the long, slow roasting process, which breaks down sulphur compounds and caramelizes natural sugars.

Basic Mayonnaise

FRESH EGGS ARE KEY to a safe mayonnaise. It will keep up to 3 days in the fridge.

Yields 2 cups (475 mL)

1	whole egg	1
1	lemon, juiced	1
dash	Dijon mustard	dash
1½ tsp.	white wine vinegar	7.5 mL
1½–2 cups	vegetable oil	360–475 mL
	salt	

Place egg, lemon juice, mustard and vinegar in a food processor or a bowl. Using a whisk or hand blender, beat mixture vigorously until it becomes pale in color. Slowly add vegetable oil in a thin stream to egg mixture until mayonnaise reaches desired thickness; the more oil added, the thicker the mayonnaise. Season to taste.

If your mayo separates, don't worry. Add lemon juice to an egg yolk, whip and gradually add back the split mayo.

Great flavors to add to mayo: basil, saffron, roasted garlic, hot peppers, capers, relish, or nut oils.

Crème Fraîche

WHILE SOUR CREAM can sometimes be substituted for crème fraîche, the sweeter flavor and fat content of crème fraîche is both necessary and desired in many dishes. If the cream turns as you make it, you will know because it smells most distinctly of blue cheese. If so, simply discard.
Yields 2 cups (475 mL)

2 cups	whipping cream	475 mL
1 Tbsp.	buttermilk	15 mL

Pour whipping cream and buttermilk into a non-reactive container (plastic or stainless steel). Stir and cover with plastic wrap. Place container into a larger container and fill space surrounding cream with hot tap water. Place in a warm space, approximately 85°F (29°C) for 24 to 36 hours until set.

Spoon off crème fraîche and drain away whey (do not mix together).

Crème fraîche is a little luxury that should be allowed in small spoonfuls and enjoyed with caviar, smoked salmon and even fresh fruit. It has that "zing" that just doesn't happen in commercial sour cream. Try it with maple syrup on your pancakes!

Roasted Peppers

ROASTED PEPPERS have become a staple in many kitchens, so much so that peeled, roasted peppers can sometimes be purchased at grocery stores. Roasting peppers is not complicated, especially if you have a barbeque.
Yields 1 cup (240 mL)

6	red, yellow or orange bell peppers	6
3 Tbsp.	olive oil	45 mL

Heat barbeque on high, or preheat oven to 400°F (200°C). Rub peppers with oil and grill until all sides are charred. If you are using the oven, place oiled peppers on a baking sheet and roast until peppers brown and deflate when removed.

Place peppers in a bowl and immediately cover with plastic wrap. Allow peppers to cool; the steam loosens the skin for easy peeling.

Peel peppers and discard seeds. Store tightly wrapped and refrigerated until required. Roasted peppers keep for up to 5 days.

APPETIZERS

Appetizers are small portions that whet the appetite but they can be served in succession to make up a full meal. You can take great care and put some finesse into this part of the meal to serve rich, full-flavored foods.

An appetizer should be something that complements, but is at the same time quite different from, the main course. These little dishes need not be overly serious; at Inn on the Twenty we like to have fun with the flavors, compositions and even names. After all, you should be able to laugh at yourself sometimes.

Foods that may be too rich in larger portions, such as paté or smoked salmon, fit in a menu perfectly as appetizers. Garnishes also play a key role in appetizers, and there are no fixed rules. Whether you garnish with fresh herbs, finely chopped red bell pepper or edible flowers, anything that has eye appeal and is edible is fair game.

Cucumber Ricotta Torte
with Smoked Salmon and Pelee Island Caviar

THIS APPETIZER can be made into individual portions using ring molds, which can be cut from 4-inch-wide (10-cm) PVC pipe. For a single torte, a cake mold can be used.

Whitefish caviar is light in texture, color and flavor. While not uncommon, whitefish caviar might not be available. Flying fish roe is an appropriate substitute.

Serves 6

2	English cucumbers	2
dash	salt	dash
dash	sugar	dash
splash	rice wine vinegar	splash
1½ lbs.	ricotta cheese	680 g
2	shallots, minced	2
2 Tbsp.	fresh basil chiffonade	30 mL
2 tsp.	finely chopped fresh mint	10 mL
2 tsp.	finely chopped fresh chives	10 mL
1 tsp.	finely chopped fresh marjoram	5 mL
	salt and pepper	
6 oz.	smoked salmon	170 g
1	2-oz. (57-g) jar Pelee Island whitefish caviar	1

Thinly slice cucumbers into rounds and toss gently with salt, sugar and a splash of vinegar. This adds flavor and softens cucumbers for easier shaping. Let cucumber sit 10 to 20 minutes.

Meanwhile, mix ricotta with chopped shallots and herbs and season to taste.

To assemble tortes, place ring molds onto a plastic wrap–lined baking sheet. Line bottoms of molds with cucumber slices, being certain to overlap slices. Using the same overlapping technique, line inside rims of molds. Spoon equal amounts of ricotta filling into each mold. Place a slice or two of smoked salmon atop ricotta. Layer overlapping cucumber slices on top of salmon.

The tortes can be prepared up to 6 hours in advance and chilled until ready to use. To serve, place each torte on individual plates using a spatula and gently slide the mold off; the moisture from the cucumbers prevents any sticking. Spoon a little caviar on top. An addition of herb stems or finely diced peppers as a garnish adds a beautiful color to the surface of the plate. Drizzle a little vinaigrette around the outside of the torte just before serving. For a lunch entrée, serve tortes on a bed of lightly dressed salad greens.

This is a very elegant-looking dish that tastes great with Sauvignon Blanc or Chardonnay. Making the tortes ahead of time ensures that you won't be pulling your hair out during your dinner party. Always try to be a "guest" at your own parties!

Tomato Tart
with Balsamic Reduction

THE GLORY OF SUMMER abounds in this tart. Any variety of tomato may be used in this recipe so long as it is very ripe.

The thought of concentrating vinegar may not sound appealing at first, but such a sweetness resonates from balsamic vinegar that it works beautifully with ripe tomatoes.

Makes 6 individual tarts or 1 large tart

1	recipe Brisée Pastry (page 124)	1
4 cups	ripe tomatoes	1 L
2	shallots, minced	2
2	cloves garlic, minced (or 5 cloves roasted)	2
¼ cup	olive oil	60 mL
¼ cup	grated parmesan	60 mL
2 Tbsp.	fresh basil chiffonade	30 mL
	salt and pepper	
1 cup	balsamic vinegar	240 mL

Preheat oven to 375°F (190°C). On a lightly floured surface, roll out brisée pastry to ¼ inch (.6 cm) thickness and line 6 individual shells or 1 large removable-bottom tart shell. Chill half an hour. Blindbake shell for 15 minutes. Remove weights and bake an additional 5 to 10 minutes, until golden brown. Allow pastry shell to cool before filling.

Increase oven temperature to 400°F (200°C). If using large tomatoes, cut into wedges, or in half if using cherry tomatoes. Toss tomatoes with remaining ingredients, except balsamic vinegar. Fill tart shell generously and bake for 12 to 15 minutes, just to warm tomatoes through and brown cheese slightly. Serve warm.

For balsamic reduction, place vinegar in a small saucepot and simmer over medium-low heat until reduced by half. Glaze will become thicker as it cools. Drizzle around the tart on each plate.

When we shot the photo of this tart at Hipple Farm, there was a flurry of activity around us; tomatoes, peaches, plums and pears being sorted, kittens being chased by the dog, and people coming by to purchase bushels of produce. We all felt lucky to get that "snapshot" of a great family farm operation.

29

Mushroom Ricotta Strudel

THIS APPETIZER IS GOOD served over salad greens or on its own. It can also serve as an accompaniment to an entrée such as Roast Pork Rack in Maple Beer Glaze or Beef Fillet in Blue Cheese Walnut Crust.

Serves 8

8 oz.	ricotta cheese	225 g
1	egg, lightly beaten	1
1/2 tsp.	salt	2.5 mL
1 tsp.	finely chopped fresh thyme	5 mL
2 Tbsp.	finely chopped fresh chives	30 mL
6 Tbsp.	unsalted butter	90 mL
2	shallots, minced	2
1 lb.	mixed mushrooms, such as button, portobello and shiitake, cleaned and sliced	455 g
2	cloves garlic, minced	2
1 tsp.	finely chopped fresh thyme	5 mL
4 Tbsp.	white wine	60 mL
	salt and pepper	
1	recipe Strudel Dough, (page 127) at room temperature	1
1/4 cup	breadcrumbs	60 mL
	1 egg with 1 Tbsp. (15 mL) water for egg wash	

Blend together ricotta, egg, salt, thyme and chives and chill until ready to use.

In a large sauté pan over medium-high heat, melt 3 Tbsp. (45 mL) butter. Sauté shallots for 2 minutes, then add mushrooms, garlic and thyme. Sauté until mushrooms are tender and all natural juices have evaporated. Add white wine, season to taste and continue to cook until wine is absorbed. Allow mixture to cool to room temperature.

Melt remaining butter and set aside.

Preheat oven to 375°F (190°C). To assemble strudel, place an old (but clean) tablecloth on a work surface, about 2 feet by 2 feet (60 cm by 60 cm). Dust cloth lightly with flour and place dough in the middle of the work surface. With flour-dusted hands, gently start pulling the dough, working from the center, and stretch it to a square the size of the work surface. Allow edges to drape over the table if needed, as this will help to anchor dough. Do not worry if dough gets a little hole—it will be covered once the strudel is rolled. Once the dough is thin enough that you could read a newspaper through it, brush entire surface with melted butter and sprinkle evenly with breadcrumbs.

At one end, spoon ricotta filling in a line about 2 inches (5 cm) wide along the length of the dough. Spoon mushroom filling on top of ricotta. Trim off the thick end pieces of dough along all 4 sides. Using the cloth, lift the end of the strudel with the filling and let the strudel roll itself up into a log. Pinch together the ends of the strudel and use the cloth to gently lift it to a parchment-lined baking sheet. If the strudel is larger than the length of the baking sheet, gently bend it to fit the pan. Brush generously with egg wash. Bake for 20 to 30 minutes until deep golden brown. Serve warm. Strudel can also be reheated in the oven.

Making strudel is a job that is easier for two or more people—do it with a friend, a mother, a lover or anyone you like. Cooking food together brings people closer. Stretch the dough by putting your hands under it, palms facing down, so the dough is resting on the backs of your hands. If you have big diamond rings, you may want to take them off. Mind you, if your diamonds are that big, hire someone to do this for you.

31

Dean Martin Shrimp Cocktail

WHAT A COMBINATION—seafood, mashed potatoes and a whiskey butter sauce! The most unlikely tastes come together to make one of Inn on the Twenty's most successful appetizers ever. This dish is convenient if mashed potatoes are already planned for the menu. Although we call for grilling the shrimp, sautéeing the shrimp is acceptable if winter weather prevents use of the barbeque. For this recipe you need 6 bamboo skewers (metal skewers tend to topple).

Serves 6

24	large uncooked tiger shrimp, peeled and deveined	24
½ cup	unsalted butter	120 mL
¼ cup	white wine	60 mL
2 Tbsp.	whiskey	30 mL
½	shallot, minced	½
	salt	
2 cups	garlic mashed potatoes (see page 102)	475 mL

Place 4 shrimp onto each skewer and chill until ready to use.

To make whiskey butter sauce, cut butter into small pieces and chill in the freezer. Place wine, whiskey and shallot into a small saucepot and simmer over low heat until reduced to 1 Tbsp. (15 mL). Remove from heat and add butter a piece at a time, stirring with a wooden spoon until melted. Return pot to low heat as needed until all butter has been incorporated. The sauce will have a thick creamy appearance. Season to taste and keep warm, but not over direct heat.

Heat grill to high and lightly oil and season shrimp. Grill just until flesh turns white (no longer translucent). To serve, spoon mashed potatoes into a martini glass, stand a shrimp skewer upright and pour butter sauce over top. A tacky cocktail umbrella makes the ideal garnish, but a couple of pickled onions would be tastier.

This dish started as a joke around a martini glass and "smashed" potatoes and still proves to be a top seller. On a cooking trip to John Folse Culinary Institute in Louisiana, we did a version of this dish with potato, lobster, scotch whiskey and pink flowers. It was called a Bay Street Lawyer and the Southerners loved it!

Facing page: Dean Martin Shrimp Cocktail (this page)

Following page: Tomato Tart with Balsamic Reduction (page 29)

32

Smoked Salmon on Potato "Crepes"
with Chive Crème Fraîche

THE APPEAL OF SMOKED SALMON paired with potato is heightened by transforming the lowly potato into a delicate crepe. Sour cream is an appropriate replacement for crème fraîche in this instance.

Serves 6 to 8

1	large Yukon Gold potato, peeled	1
¾ tsp.	salt	4 mL
1	whole egg	1
3 Tbsp.	all purpose flour	45 mL
½ cup	2% milk	120 mL
2 Tbsp.	unsalted butter, melted	30 mL
½ cup	Crème Fraîche (see page 25)	120 mL
2 Tbsp.	finely chopped fresh chives	30 mL
6–8 oz.	smoked salmon	170–225 g

Grate potato very finely and sprinkle immediately with salt to prevent browning. Combine potato well with egg, flour, milk and melted butter. Heat a Teflon or crepe pan over medium-high heat and grease lightly. Drop in spoonfuls of crepe mixture and spread thinly around pan. Cook crepe until top surface is dry and then turn to brown other side for 1 or 2 minutes. Crepes can be made smaller (3 per person) or larger (1 per person) and stored in the refrigerator until ready to use. Simply rewarm in a low oven, 250°F (120°C).

Combine crème fraîche with chives. To serve, fold slices of smoked salmon over potato crepes and spoon crème fraîche over salmon.

❦ *This is a very versatile recipe for cocktail parties, a dinner course or even part of a champagne brunch. Top with caviar for an extra treat.*

33

Facing page: Smoked Salmon on Potato "Crepes" with Chive Crème Fraîche (this page)

Preceding page: Mushroom "Cappuccino" Bisque (page 41)

Terrine of Salmon, Scallops and Monkfish
with Basil Mousseline

THIS TERRINE can be sliced thinly and placed on toast points. The Basil Mousseline is a light-tasting accompaniment that adds a summery flair to this delicate terrine. Do prepare this a day ahead, as the terrine needs time to set.

Serves 12

1½ cups	whipping cream	360 mL
2 slices	white bread, crusts removed, torn into pieces	2 slices
1 lb.	fresh salmon, skin and pinbones removed	455 g
4 oz.	shrimp, peeled and deveined	113 g
2	eggs	2
3 Tbsp.	white wine	45 mL
	salt and pepper	
4 oz.	sea scallops, cut into quarters	113 g
4 oz.	monkfish, diced	113 g

Combine ½ the cream with bread. Allow bread to soak and set aside.

Place salmon and shrimp in a food processor and blend for 30 seconds. Add eggs and bread-cream mixture and blend until smooth. While blending, add white wine, remaining cream, salt and pepper.

To test seasoning, bring a small pan of water to a simmer and drop a small spoonful of mixture into it. Let poach until cooked. Allow to cool and taste. Adjust seasoning if necessary.

Remove terrine base from processor and fold in scallops and monkfish.

Preheat oven to 300°F (150°C). Line a lightly oiled loaf pan or terrine mold with parchment paper, leaving some paper overhanging. Fill mold with terrine mix until it reaches the level top. Fold over extra parchment paper and cover top with foil. Place mold in roasting pan filled with 1½ inches (4 cm) boiling water. Cook terrine for 30 minutes, until terrine registers an internal temperature of 150°F (65°C). Allow terrine to cool and refrigerate for at least 12 hours before cutting. Serve with Basil Mousseline.

Basil Mousseline

½ cup	whipping cream	120 mL
1 cup	mayonnaise (see page 24)	240 mL
2 Tbsp.	fresh basil chiffonade	30 mL

Whip cream to soft peaks. Fold in mayonnaise and add basil. This can be prepared a few hours ahead of time, to allow flavors to meld.

A delicate seafood terrine makes a sophisticated start to an elegant meal and goes nicely with a delicious Niagara Riesling or Gewurtztraminer.

This recipe comes from an expert on pâtés and terrines, Luther Miller, one of the nicest guys in the world.

Terrine of Chicken and Quail
with Pistachios and Apricots

TERRINES ARE IMPRESSIVE because they appear to be more difficult to make than they really are. If quail is not available for this recipe, you can substitute diced chicken breast. *Serves 10 to 12*

3 oz.	pistachios, shelled	85 g
12 oz.	quail breasts	340 g
1½ slices	white bread, cubed	1½ slices
1 cup	whipping cream	240 mL
1½ lbs.	boneless, skinless chicken	680 g
2	eggs	2
¼ cup	white wine	60 mL
¼ cup	dried apricots, diced	60 mL
¼ cup	dried pitted prunes, diced	60 mL
	salt and pepper	
5 oz.	prosciutto ham, thinly sliced	140 g

Soak pistachios in hot water for 20 minutes. Strain, peel husks from pistachios and set aside.

In a sauté pan over medium-high heat, sear lightly seasoned quail breasts on both sides just until browned, not cooked through. Remove quail from heat and chill.

Soak bread in a bowl with ½ the cream. Blend chicken breasts in a food processor for 30 seconds. Add bread mixture, eggs and a touch of salt and pepper. Blend for 1 minute. While puréeing, add white wine and remaining cream and blend until smooth.

To test seasoning, bring a small pan of water to a simmer. Drop a small spoonful of mixture into the pan and poach until cooked through. Allow to cool and taste. Adjust seasoning as desired, remembering to retaste until satisfied.

Remove mixture from processor and fold in pistachios, apricots and prunes. Chill at least 1 hour before building terrine.

Preheat oven to 325°F (165°C). Line a lightly oiled loaf pan or terrine mold with parchment paper, leaving some paper overhanging. Line the mold with slices of prosciutto, overlapping slices until the mold is completely covered and some slices are overhanging. Spoon ⅓ of the chicken mixture into the mold, spreading to the edges with a spatula. Arrange ½ of the quail breasts onto the chicken mixture. Spread another ⅓ of the chicken over the quail breasts. Arrange remaining quail and spread with the last of the chicken mixture. Fold prosciutto slices over and cover with parchment paper. Wrap terrine with foil.

Place terrine in a roasting pan and pour in 1½ inches (4 cm) boiling water. Cook for 45 minutes, until internal temperature of terrine is 165°F (74°C). Cool terrine and refrigerate overnight before slicing.

Cooking time will depend on the size of your mold. An instant-read analog or digital thermometer will ensure the terrine is fully cooked.

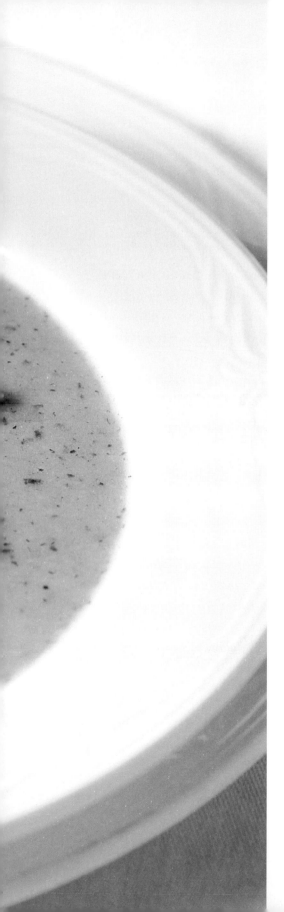

SOUPS

37

"It is to a dinner what a portico or a peristyle is to a building; that is to say, it is not only the first part of it, but it must be devised in such a manner as to set the tone of the whole banquet, in the same way as the overture of an opera announces the subject of the work." —GRIMOD DE LA REYNIÈRE

Soup can be part of an elaborate dinner, half of a lunch or a meal in itself. There are thin clear soups, creamy ones and thick ones (generally made with potatoes or squash).

Bisques are much easier to make with a hand blender: instead of fussing with a food processor and puréeing soup in batches, you can simply place the blender wand directly in the pot and—voilà—bisque.

A nice treat during the summer heat is a chilled soup—think of it as air conditioning for your insides. What could be better before a grilled steak than an icy gazpacho that catches the taste of summer tomatoes at their best?

Ideally, serve hot soup in heated bowls and chilled soup in frozen ones. You can also be creative in the way you dress it up—ladle chilled soup from a hollowed-out watermelon, or serve an autumn bisque in seeded mini pumpkins.

Following are some of the most popular soups from Inn on the Twenty that encompass all seasons and use ingredients you can find at your local market. We find that a great meal at home can often be nothing more than a good homemade soup with some bread, cheese, cold cuts and pickles.

Sweet Pepper Soup
with Chervil Cream

THIS VIBRANTLY COLORED soup can be made with red, yellow or orange peppers—the effect is the same. Mixing colors is not recommended, however, as a muddied color will result.

Chervil is a delicate herb that accents the soup nicely, but is not always available. Any mild herb, such as mint, basil, lemon balm or even thyme can be substituted.

Serves 6 to 8

1 Tbsp.	vegetable oil	15 mL
1	medium onion, diced	1
1	rib celery, chopped	1
1	clove garlic, minced	1
4	red bell peppers, seeded and diced	4
1	Yukon gold potato, peeled and diced	1
½ cup	white wine	120 mL
4 cups	Chicken Stock (page 18)	950 mL
1 tsp.	chopped fresh thyme	5 mL
	salt and pepper	
½ cup	sour cream	120 mL
2 Tbsp.	fresh chervil, chopped	30 mL

In a medium saucepot, heat oil and sauté onion and celery over medium heat until onions are translucent, about 5 minutes. Add garlic and peppers and continue to sauté until peppers are just softened.

Add diced potato, white wine, stock and thyme. Bring to a simmer and cook until potatoes are tender. Purée soup with a hand blender or in a food processor. Strain. Return to heat and season to taste.

Whisk sour cream until smooth and fold in chervil. To serve, ladle soup into cups and spoon sour cream over top.

Inn on the Twenty is near so many different food producers. Some are backyard hobby farmers and others are state-of-the-art greenhouse operations. We use literally tons of peppers from a huge hydroponic greenhouse called St. David's, which was under the direction of our dearly departed friend, Andy Olsthoorn, who regularly enjoyed his own peppers prepared in many fashions at the restaurant.

38

Winter and Summer Tomato Soup

TOMATO SOUP is a seasonless treat but, unfortunately, the best tomatoes are limited to summer. Two variations of this recipe, each with their own character, allow you to enjoy a classic any time of year.
Serves 6 to 8

2 Tbsp.	vegetable oil	30 mL
1	onion, diced	1
1	rib celery, chopped	1
2	cloves garlic, minced	2
2 lbs.	fresh ripe tomatoes, diced	900 g
	or	
1	28-oz. (796-mL) can diced tomatoes	1
¼ cup	sundried tomatoes, chopped	60 mL
3 cups	Chicken Stock (page 18)	720 mL
1 tsp.	fresh thyme, chopped	5 mL
½ tsp.	chopped fresh rosemary (winter)	2.5 mL
	or	
¼ cup	fresh basil, chopped (summer)	60 mL
	salt and pepper	
¼ cup	whipping cream	60 mL

In a medium saucepot, heat oil and sauté onion and celery over medium heat until translucent, about 5 minutes.

Add garlic and sauté 1 minute more. Add tomatoes, chicken stock and herbs, except basil, and simmer for 20 minutes.

Purée soup with a hand blender or in a food processor. Strain. Return to heat and season to taste. If using basil, add with cream and return soup just to a simmer before serving.

As much as summer tomatoes can't be beat, a good-quality tinned tomato creates a summer memory in the dead of winter.

Never refrigerate tomatoes! Allow them to ripen at room temperature and eat them just before they want to collapse. At the restaurant, we call this soup "Field Heat" in September because we get tomatoes from farmers, wash them and make soup before the heat of the sun has left them.

Yellow Gazpacho
with Tomato Granita

THE COLOR CONTRAST of yellow gazpacho and icy tomato granita looks beautiful on a summer table. Gazpacho is convenient to serve for a party since it can be prepared in advance and, in fact, tastes better given the time to rest and let the flavors meld. Adding cooked baby shrimp to this soup as a garnish makes it even more delightful.
Serves 6 to 8

½ cup	chopped sweet onion	120 mL
1	English cucumber, peeled and chopped	1
1	clove garlic, minced	1
2	yellow peppers, seeded and chopped	2
2	lemons, juiced	2
2 cups	cold water	475 mL
2 Tbsp.	finely chopped fresh basil	30 mL
1 Tbsp.	finely chopped fresh chives	15 mL
1 Tbsp.	finely chopped fresh chervil (optional)	15 mL
½ Tbsp.	finely chopped fresh mint	7.5 mL
½ tsp.	finely chopped fresh thyme	2.5 mL
dash	hot pepper sauce	dash
	salt and pepper	

In a food processor or in a bowl using a hand blender, purée together first 6 ingredients. Let mixture rest for 20 minutes to allow natural water from vegetables to come out. Purée again.

Stir in herbs and season to taste. Chill until ready to serve.

Tomato Granita

1 cup	tomatoes, peeled and diced	240 mL
1	green onion, diced	1
1	clove garlic, minced	1
2 Tbsp.	lemon juice	30 mL
1 Tbsp.	chopped fresh basil	15 mL
1 Tbsp.	chopped fresh coriander	15 mL
dash	hot pepper sauce	dash
	salt and pepper	

In a food processor or with a hand blender, purée all ingredients and place in freezer. After 1 hour, gently stir ice. Let granita rest in the freezer for at least 4 hours.

To serve, scrape up granules with a fork to loosen. Granita may then be scooped into bowls of gazpacho.

 Gazpacho is such a great patio or cottage treat because it can be made a day ahead and simply poured into bowls and served as a first course or as a lunch with cold cuts, cheese and bread. I think a glass of Cave Spring Rosé is a perfect way to round out the flavors of this soup.

40

Mushroom "Cappuccino" Bisque

THE CHOICE OF MUSHROOMS is the key to a flavorful soup. While it is not necessary to use the most expensive mushrooms, the addition of a few portobello and/or shiitake mushrooms to a base of button mushrooms heightens the flavor. The use of potato as a thickener reduces the necessity for cream and also generates a smooth consistency.
Serves 6 to 8

2 Tbsp.	vegetable oil	30 mL
1	onion, peeled and diced	1
1	rib celery, diced	1
2	cloves garlic, minced	2
2 lbs.	mixed mushrooms, including button, crimini, portobello, shiitake and oyster	900 g
1 cup	white wine	240 mL
4 cups	Light Chicken Stock (page 18)	950 mL
1 tsp.	chopped fresh thyme	5 mL
1	Yukon Gold potato, peeled and diced	1
	salt and pepper	
1/2 cup	whipping cream (optional)	120 mL

In a medium saucepot over medium heat, sauté onion and celery in vegetable oil until onions are translucent, about 5 minutes. Add garlic and mushrooms and continue to sauté for 10 minutes more.

Add white wine, stock, thyme and potato and bring to a simmer. Cook until potato is tender. Purée soup with a hand blender or in a food processor. Return to pot and season to taste. If desired, add cream, return just to a simmer and serve.

"Cappuccino" Cream

At Inn on the Twenty, we add a dash of truffle oil to the cream. A touch of brandy or chopped chives would also be very tasty.

1/2 cup	whipping cream	120 mL

Whip cream to soft peaks and add desired flavoring. Spoon over soup. The cream will melt slightly and create the look of foamed milk.

Nothing says "woodsy" like the rich flavor of a mushroom soup, especially on those first cool autumn days. Unless the mushrooms are really dirty, you can just brush them clean with a small (unused) paintbrush or a terry towel.

Serve this soup in oversized coffee cups to mimic the look of cappuccino with a grating of black pepper on the cream to look like cocoa powder.

41

Corn Chowder
with Sweet Pepper and Thyme

THIS HAS BEEN one of Inn on the Twenty's most popular soup recipe requests and deservedly so. Such basic flavors combine to make a soup that, with a slice of grain bread or potato bread, makes a meal on its own.
Serves 6 to 8

4	strips bacon, diced	4
1	onion, diced	1
1	rib celery, diced	1
1	carrot, peeled and diced	1
1	red bell pepper, seeded and diced	1
2 Tbsp.	unsalted butter	30 mL
2 Tbsp.	all purpose flour	30 mL
2 cups	Chicken Stock (pages 18, 19)	475 mL
2 cups	2% milk	475 mL
4	cobs corn, kernels removed	4
	or	
1½ cups	corn kernels, fresh or frozen	360 mL
2 tsp.	chopped fresh thyme	10 mL
1	Yukon Gold potato, peeled and diced	1
	salt and pepper	

In a medium saucepot, cook diced bacon over medium-high heat until crispy. Remove bacon from pan, but leave fat. Allow pan to cool to medium heat and add onion, celery and carrot and sauté until tender, about 5 minutes. Add pepper and cook for an additional 5 minutes. Remove from pan and set aside.

In the same saucepan, melt butter over low to medium heat. Add flour and stir with a wooden spoon for 5 minutes, until flour takes on a slightly nutty aroma but doesn't color. Using a whisk, gradually add chicken stock, whisking constantly until smooth. Whisk in milk and turn heat up to medium. Add bacon, sautéed vegetables, corn and thyme. Add diced potato and simmer chowder for 20 minutes, until potatoes are cooked through. Season to taste before serving.

This is a very versatile recipe that shows off that sweet buttery flavor of corn when it's at its best. If you are a vegetarian, simply omit the bacon and use vegetable stock. If you wish to avoid wheat gluten, skip the flour, then purée about one-third of the solids and add back into the soup for body.

Ham and Barley Soup
with Parmesan Crostini

COMFORT FOOD at its best. This soup can be made with a leftover ham bone or with diced ham. The barley cooked into the broth naturally thickens the soup. Be sure to rinse your barley well before adding to the soup to keep the broth clear. This is definitely one of those soups that tastes better served the next day.
Serves 6 to 8

2 Tbsp.	vegetable oil	30 mL
1	onion, diced	1
2	ribs celery, diced	2
2	carrots, peeled and diced	2
6 cups	Light Chicken Stock (page 18)	1.5 L
1	ham bone	1
2 cups	diced ham (3 cups/720 mL if you aren't using the ham bone)	475 mL
1/2 cup	barley, rinsed	120 mL
2 tsp.	chopped fresh thyme	10 mL
	salt and pepper	

In a medium saucepot (or larger if you have a large ham bone), heat oil and sauté onion, celery and carrot until tender, about 5 minutes. Add chicken stock, ham bone and ham and bring to a simmer. Add barley and thyme and gently simmer until barley is cooked, 45 minutes to 1 hour. Season to taste.

Parmesan Crostini

8	thin slices of French stick (day-old is preferable)	8
3 Tbsp.	olive oil	45 mL
3 Tbsp.	grated parmesan	45 mL
1/2 tsp.	finely chopped fresh thyme	2.5 mL

Preheat oven to 400°F (200°C). Lightly brush both sides of bread slices with olive oil and place on a baking sheet. Combine parmesan and thyme and sprinkle over bread. Toast bread in oven until brown and crisp.

For a truly Canadian experience, you should eat this soup with a grilled cheese sandwich, preferably after shoveling snow and, of course, wearing a hockey jersey.

Butternut Squash Bisque
with Maple Sage Cream

ROASTING THE SQUASH for this recipe concentrates the flavor and brings out a tasty sweetness in the soup, but it's not mandatory for a delicious result. Butternut squash has a smooth texture that lends itself well to a bisque, more than any other squash variety. Pumpkin may be a close substitute, but fresh pumpkin is strongly recommended if you must use an alternative to squash.

Serves 6 to 8

1 lb.	butternut squash	455 g
2 Tbsp.	vegetable oil	30 mL
1	onion, diced	1
1	rib celery, diced	1
1	carrot, peeled and diced	1
1	clove garlic, minced (or 3 cloves roasted)	1
4 cups	Light Chicken Stock (page 18)	950 mL
1	Yukon Gold potato, peeled and diced	1
1½ tsp.	chopped fresh thyme	7.5 mL
dash	ground nutmeg	dash
¼ cup	whipping cream (optional) salt and pepper	60 mL

Preheat oven to 350°F (175°C). Cut squash in half lengthwise and scoop out seeds. Place flesh-side down on a buttered baking sheet and roast for 30 to 40 minutes, until tender. Allow squash to cool and peel off skin.

In a medium saucepot, heat oil and sauté onion, celery and carrot until tender, about 5 minutes. Add garlic and sauté 1 minute. Add chicken stock, squash, potato, thyme and nutmeg and simmer until potato is tender, 20 to 30 minutes.

Purée using a hand blender or a food processor. Strain. Return to heat and add cream. Season to taste and bring just to a simmer before serving.

Maple Sage Cream

½ cup	whipping cream	120 mL
1 Tbsp.	pure maple syrup	15 mL
1 tsp.	finely chopped fresh sage	5 mL

Whip cream to soft peaks and fold in maple syrup and sage. Spoon over bowls of soup immediately before serving.

❧ *The fall colors of Niagara are truly beautiful, and as soon as it begins to cool down, we put down our barbeque tongs and lean towards rich soups and stews and slow-roasted meats.*

In peeling many varieties of squash, a sticky film is left on your hands. To avoid this, wear a pair of disposable latex gloves, which can be purchased at drugstores. These also come in handy when peeling beets or garlic, or when working with raw chicken.

Caramelized Onion Cream Soup

THE "CREAM" in this recipe title is almost a misnomer since the creaminess of the soup is attained not so much by cream (which can be omitted from the recipe altogether) but by the smooth texture of blended caramelized onions.

Serves 6 to 8

2 Tbsp.	unsalted butter	30 mL
4	onions, peeled and julienned	4
2	cloves garlic (or 5 cloves roasted)	2
1 cup	white wine	240 mL
2 Tbsp.	sherry	30 mL
4 cups	Dark Chicken Stock (page 19)	950 mL
1	Yukon Gold potato, peeled and diced	1
1 tsp.	chopped fresh thyme	5 mL
1 tsp.	chopped fresh rosemary	5 mL
1/2 cup	whipping cream (optional)	120 mL
	salt and pepper	

In a medium heavy-bottomed saucepot, heat butter over medium-low heat and add onions. Using a wooden spoon, stir onions regularly until they soften and begin to take on color. This will take 20 to 30 minutes. Once onions have a little color, add garlic and 1/3 of the wine. Continue stirring until wine is absorbed (pan will deglaze and onions will take on a deeper brown color). Add remaining wine by thirds and stir until it is absorbed.

Add sherry, stock, potato and herbs and bring soup to a simmer. Cook until potatoes are tender. Purée using a hand blender or food processor. Strain. Return soup to heat, add cream and season to taste. Bring just to a simmer before serving.

For all you poor souls who have suffered through the brutal attempts at French Onion Soup, choked with MSG and tongue-tied by looms of stringy cheese, this soup is a knight in shining armor. The onion is a lowly character who, with some coaxing, turns out to be a gustatory celebration with fireworks of sherry and fresh thyme. You can leave the bottle uncorked, thank you; the sherry goes nicely with the soup!

Roast Parsnip Soup
with Honeyed Hazelnuts and Brandy Crème Fraîche

THIS SOUP APPEARED on our Thanksgiving menu one year and the response was overwhelming. Our guests were impressed with how delicious a parsnip could be! This recipe brings out the sweet spiciness of the underrated root vegetable and, with the accompaniments of hazelnuts and brandy crème fraîche, elevates it to a much less humble status.

Serves 6 to 8

1½ lbs.	parsnips, peeled and roughly chopped	680 g
4 Tbsp.	vegetable oil	60 mL
1	onion, diced	1
1	rib celery, chopped	1
1	clove garlic (or 3 roasted)	1
½ cup	white wine	120 mL
6 cups	Dark Chicken Stock (page 19) (light is acceptable)	1.5 L
1 tsp.	chopped fresh thyme	5 mL
1 tsp.	chopped fresh sage	5 mL
	salt and pepper	
¼ cup	whipping cream (optional)	60 mL

Preheat oven to 350°F (175°C). Toss parsnips in 2 Tbsp. (30 mL) of vegetable oil and place on a baking sheet. Roast for 20 minutes or until fork-tender.

Meanwhile, in a medium saucepot, heat remaining oil and sauté onion and celery until translucent, about 5 minutes. Add garlic and sauté 1 minute more. Add white wine, stock, parsnips and herbs and simmer for 20 to 30 minutes. Purée and strain. Return soup to pot, stir in the cream, if using, and season to taste. Return soup just to a simmer and serve with Honeyed Hazelnuts and Brandy Crème Fraîche.

Honeyed Hazelnuts

| ²/₃ cup | whole hazelnuts, roughly chopped | 160 mL |
| 1 Tbsp. | honey | 15 mL |

Preheat oven to 325°F (165°C). Place hazelnuts on a greased tray and bake for 10 minutes. Allow to cool 10 minutes and then toss nuts in honey and return to tray. Bake 5 to 10 minutes more until honey has caramelized onto hazelnuts. Allow to cool completely before crumbling over soup.

Brandy Crème Fraîche

| ³/₄ cup | Crème Fraîche (page 25) | 180 mL |
| 1 Tbsp. | brandy | 15 mL |

Combine crème fraîche and brandy and keep chilled until ready to spoon over soup. Sour cream can be substituted for crème fraîche.

As much as soup is not classically served with wine, we find that Gewurtztraminer goes nicely with parsnip. Gewurtztraminer has a floral character and a "spice" that is almost like the scent of a baker's cupboard. Similarly, parsnip has a faint aroma of mace, nutmeg and brown sugar, which is a great background for the honeyed hazelnuts and brandy crème fraîche.

47

SALADS

These are salads that go beyond lettuce and dressing to make a great lunch on their own, or a part of dinner. Don't be afraid to experiment and use your favorite ingredients in one of our vinaigrette recipes. Warm salads are a great way to use leftover roasts or cheese after a family meal.

At Inn on the Twenty, we tend to compose several complementary flavors that are seasonally appropriate. In the spring, we just can't get enough asparagus, the late summer brings us the very best tomatoes, and as cool weather approaches, it just makes sense to reach for apples, walnuts, blue cheese and bitter greens.

Use your imagination and be creative in presenting salads—don't always toss everything in a bowl. Arrange things on a plate, platter or even a mirror to show off the natural beauty of the fresh ingredients.

49

Endive and Field Green Salad
in Lovage Vinaigrette

LOVAGE HAS A STRONG celery flavor to it, which is why it is most commonly used to enhance soups and stuffings. However, within a vinaigrette, lovage complements the "green" flavor of mixed lettuces and balances well with endive.

Serves 6 to 8

3 Tbsp.	sherry vinegar	45 mL
1	shallot, minced	1
1/2 tsp.	Dijon mustard	2.5 ml
1/4 tsp. each	salt and pepper	1.2 mL
6 Tbsp.	grapeseed or canola oil	90 mL
1 Tbsp.	finely chopped lovage leaves	15 mL
2 Tbsp.	water	30 mL
1	head Belgian endive	1
6 cups	mixed greens such as romaine, boston, radicchio, frisée and escarole	1.5 L

In a bowl, whisk together vinegar, shallot, mustard, salt and pepper until well incorporated. Slowly drizzle in oil while whisking constantly. Add lovage and whisk in water.

This vinaigrette can be made ahead of time and refrigerated—just whisk before dressing greens.

Arrange endive spears around platter or individual salad plates. Wash, dry and tear greens into bite-size pieces and place them in center of platter or plates. Drizzle vinaigrette atop greens.

Lovage is not commonly found in groceries but is easy to grow in your garden. In its place, use flat leaf parsley and light-colored celery leaves from the inner stalks to achieve a similar flavor.

Grilled Summer Vegetables
on Goat Cheese Fondant

THIS SALAD CAN BE SERVED warm off the grill, or at room temperature. When grilling vegetables, only brush them lightly with oil—vegetables will soak up as much oil as you give them, and it will serve only to char them. *Serves 6 to 8*

½	large eggplant, sliced lengthwise	½
2	medium zucchini, sliced lengthwise	2
2	red or yellow bell peppers, seeded and sectioned	2
6	green onions, trimmed	6
6	portobello mushroom caps	6

Dressing

2 Tbsp.	balsamic vinegar	30 mL
6 Tbsp.	extra virgin olive oil	90 mL
¼ cup	fresh basil chiffonade	60 mL
	salt and pepper	

Goat Cheese Fondant

½ cup	mild goat cheese	120 mL
¼ cup	half-and-half cream	60 ml
	salt and pepper	

Preheat grill to moderately high heat. Lightly brush oil on vegetables, just to prevent sticking. Grill vegetables evenly on both sides until softened. Do not overcook on the grill, as the vegetables will continue cooking after they have been removed. Slice vegetables into smaller pieces, if desired.

In a large bowl, whisk together all ingredients for dressing and toss gently with grilled vegetables. Allow vegetables to marinate for 10 minutes.

In a small saucepot over low heat, melt together goat cheese, cream, salt and pepper, stirring occasionally.

To serve, arrange grilled vegetables on a platter or individual plates and drizzle fondant over them with a spoon.

The term "fondant" generally refers to a thin white icing that decorates sweet rolls and pastries. The look of the goat cheese dressing is similar to fondant and can be drizzled in any shape or design you choose. The grilled vegetable salad is great either right after cooking or the next day as a cold dish.

Roasted Pepper Salad
in Marjoram Dressing

THE VIBRANT COLOR of this salad is matched by its outstanding flavor. The natural sweetness of roasted peppers is complemented by fresh marjoram. This is an ideal summer salad or first course to a robust Italian-style entrée. *Serves 6 to 8*

3 Tbsp.	white wine vinegar	45 mL
1 tsp.	Dijon mustard	5 mL
$\frac{1}{4}$ tsp. each	salt and pepper	1.2 mL
6 Tbsp.	extra virgin olive oil	90 mL
1 Tbsp.	finely chopped fresh marjoram	15 mL
2 Tbsp.	finely chopped green onion or chives	30 mL
2 Tbsp.	water	30 mL
4	red and/or yellow bell peppers, roasted, peeled and julienned (see page 25)	4
6 cups	mesclun mix salad greens	1.5 L

For dressing, whisk together vinegar, mustard, salt and pepper. Slowly drizzle in oil while whisking constantly. Add marjoram and green onion and whisk in water.

Toss half of the dressing over roasted peppers and let sit 10 minutes. Arrange greens on a platter or individual salad plates. Drizzle greens with remaining dressing and arrange roasted peppers on top.

52

Blue Cheese and Apple Salad
with Boston Lettuce and Walnuts

FOR A BALANCE in flavor, do use apples that are high in acidity; we prefer Mutsu apples, but Macintosh or Granny Smith apples serve the purpose well.
Serves 6 to 8

2	lemons, juiced	2
½ tsp.	Dijon mustard	2.5 mL
1	shallot, minced	1
¼ tsp. each	salt and pepper	1.2 mL
dash	honey	dash
6 Tbsp.	grapeseed or canola oil	90 mL
1 tsp.	finely chopped fresh tarragon	5 mL
2 Tbsp.	water	30 mL
1 head	Boston lettuce	1
2	Mutsu apples	2
6–8 oz.	blue cheese	170–225 g
⅔ cup	walnut pieces, lightly toasted	160 mL

In a bowl, whisk together lemon juice, mustard, shallot, salt and pepper, and honey. Slowly drizzle in oil, whisking constantly. Add tarragon and whisk in water. Set dressing aside.

Separate Boston lettuce into leaves, wash well and dry. Arrange the leaves on a platter or individual salad plates. Leaving skin on, cut apple into thin slices and arrange them over lettuce. Crumble blue cheese over salad and sprinkle with walnuts. Drizzle vinaigrette over salad and serve.

This salad requires no vinegar, making it wine-friendly and appropriate as a course before or after an entrée.

Beet, Grapefruit and Parmesan Salad

THIS WINE-FRIENDLY composed salad is easy to assemble and the contrasting colors and flavors create a palatable dish for the eyes and mouth. This contrast in flavor replaces a vinaigrette. A simple drizzle of olive oil ties the components together.

Serves 6 to 8

2 cups	mesclun mix salad greens	475 mL
4	medium beets, cooked, peeled and cut into wedges or slices	4
2	red grapefruits	2
2 oz.	parmesan cheese wedge	57 g
3 Tbsp.	extra virgin olive oil	45 mL
	salt and pepper	

Arrange greens on a platter or individual salad plates. Arrange beets on top of greens.

To section grapefruit, slice top and bottom off fruit. Slice peel away from fruit, exposing the flesh. With a paring knife, separate segments from membrane and arrange over salad.

Using a vegetable peeler or wood rasp, shave parmesan over salad. The cheese comes away almost in curls. Drizzle salad with olive oil and sprinkle lightly with salt and freshly cracked black pepper.

We serve this salad before roasted meats or chicken at home. The sweetness of the beets, the salt of the cheese, and the acidity of the citrus balance each other nicely and go very well with Cave Spring Off-Dry Riesling.

Prosciutto and Pear Salad
with Asiago and Peppered Almonds

THE PEPPERED ALMONDS that garnish this dish make a tasty snack on their own or with cocktails; simply double this recipe to make extra and store unrefrigerated in an airtight container. The almonds can be stored indefinitely but they probably won't last long. They are certainly popular with the staff of Inn on the Twenty!

Serves 6 to 8

1 cup	whole unblanched almonds	240 mL
2 Tbsp.	salt	30 mL
¼ cup	sugar	60 mL
1 cup	water	240 mL
2 Tbsp.	honey	30 mL
1 Tbsp.	freshly cracked black pepper	15 mL
6–8 oz.	thinly sliced prosciutto	170–225 g
3	Bartlett or Bosc pears	3
4 oz.	Asiago cheese, finely grated	113 g
	extra virgin olive oil	

To make peppered almonds, preheat oven to 350°F (175°C). Place nuts, salt, sugar and water in a small saucepot and bring to a simmer. Cook for 10 minutes, then drain away liquid. Place nuts on a foil-lined baking sheet and toast for 10 to 15 minutes, stirring occasionally. Allow the almonds to cool, then toss with honey and black pepper and return to oven for 7 to 10 minutes, until honey becomes glazed onto nuts.

To assemble, arrange prosciutto in curls or flat slices on a platter or individual salad plates. Leaving skins on, thinly slice pears and arrange the slices over prosciutto. Sprinkle with grated Asiago and lightly drizzle with olive oil. Sprinkle peppered almonds over top and serve.

Prosciutto is an Italian salt-cured ham native to the Parma region that recently has been allowed as an import into Canada (it was banned in the past as it is not fully cooked). There are good-quality domestic prosciuttos available and at the restaurant we order them 45 at a time from an Italian friend's father who makes them from a secret family recipe.

Warm Mushroom Salad
with Sundried Tomato Vinaigrette

56

THIS SALAD IS SO POPULAR that it cannot be removed from the menu. The simplicity in its preparation does not suggest the complexity of its flavor, which perhaps is why it is also one of our most popular recipe requests.
Serves 6 to 8

6 Tbsp.	olive oil	90 mL
2	shallots, minced	2
1 lb.	mixed mushrooms, including button, crimini, portobello, shiitake and oyster, cleaned and sliced	455 g
2	cloves garlic, minced	2
1 tsp.	finely chopped fresh thyme	5 mL
4 Tbsp.	sundried tomatoes, (reconstituted if not oil-packed) and chopped	60 mL
3 Tbsp.	balsamic vinegar	45 mL
	salt and pepper	
4 Tbsp.	finely chopped green onions	60 mL
6 cups	mesclun mix salad greens	1.5 L

Heat a large sauté pan over medium-high heat. Add 3 Tbsp. (45 mL) of oil and shallots and sauté for 1 minute. Add mushrooms, garlic and thyme and sauté until mushrooms soften. Add sundried tomatoes, vinegar and salt and pepper to taste. Cook for 2 minutes.

Finish mushrooms with remaining olive oil and toss in green onions. Spoon immediately onto salad greens and serve.

Using a mix of mushrooms provides differences in size, texture and taste. The mix is your choice, but earthier-tasting mushrooms such as shiitake and portobello are recommended. Try whatever is available and fresh at your market.

If your mushrooms are dirty, simply brush them off with a dry towel. If they are very dirty, place them in a strainer and rinse with cold water.

Truffled White Beans
with Spinach, Bacon and Lemon

THIS WINTRY SALAD is hearty enough to serve as a lunch entrée. The peasant flavor of white beans is made elegant through the addition of truffle oil, but if truffle oil is not available, the dish will not suffer.

If cooking the beans from dry, try cooking them in stock or adding a halved onion to the liquid; the flavor difference is substantial.

Serves 6 to 8

4	strips bacon, diced	4
2	shallots, minced	2
2 cups	cooked white beans	475 mL
2 tsp.	finely chopped fresh thyme	10 mL
1½	lemons, juiced	1½
	salt and pepper	
2 Tbsp.	olive oil	30 mL
1 tsp.	truffle oil	5 mL
4 cups	baby leaf spinach	1 L

In a medium sauté pan, cook bacon over moderate heat until crispy. Remove bacon but leave fat. Add shallots and sauté 1 minute. Add beans, thyme and lemon juice and warm them through. If necessary, add a splash of water or stock to keep beans from sticking. Return bacon to pan. Season to taste and add olive and truffle oils.

Arrange spinach greens on a platter or individual plates and spoon warm beans on top. Serve warm.

Always sort dry beans first to make sure there are no pebbles; there's always at least one. Soak dry beans overnight or, if time prevents, soak them in hot water for an hour. Don't add salt to the cooking water until the very end. Remember— dry beans more than double in volume once cooked.

I like the "high/low" dishes like this one with inexpensive beans and pricey truffle. Try some on your own: lobster and mashed potato or perogies with smoked salmon, crème fraîche and caviar.

57

Michael Olson

FISH AND SHELLFISH

Niagara is surrounded by water, with Lake Ontario to the north, Lake Erie to the south and the mighty Niagara River at the eastern border of Ontario and New York. Yet local fish production is very low, limited to rainbow trout, perch and pickerel, so we've had to do something called "Niagaracize." When we bring in a product from outside of our area we try to use as many local ingredients with it as possible to acclimate it to our part of the world.

The recipes that follow show a selection of fish and shellfish prepared using different methods. Do bear in mind the recipes have been chosen to include products that can be found across the country.

Sea Scallops
on Apricot Butter Sauce

THIS DISH ALSO MAKES a great appetizer, using one scallop per person. Using a heavy-bottomed fry pan or well-seasoned cast iron pan will result in an attractive and well-caramelized searing of the scallops, without the need for a great deal of oil in the pan. The mildness of apricots brings out the natural sweetness in the scallops, which can be further complemented by serving Off-Dry Riesling.

Sea salt is added after the scallops have been cooked, to avoid drawing out juices while cooking.

Serves 6

1	shallot, minced	1
4	fresh apricots, pitted and diced	4
$2/3$ cup	white wine	160 mL
	juice of 1 lemon	
$1/2$ cup	unsalted butter, cut into small pieces and chilled	120 mL
	salt and pepper	
$1/2$ tsp.	sugar or honey	2.5 mL
2 Tbsp.	vegetable oil	30 mL
18	large fresh sea scallops	18
	sea salt and pepper	

For the sauce, place shallot, apricots, wine and lemon juice in a small saucepot and simmer until liquid is reduced by $1/2$. Reduce heat to low and gradually add cold butter, a piece at a time, while stirring, until all the butter is incorporated. Season with salt and pepper and sugar or honey. Remove from heat and set aside.

To sear scallops, place a heavy-bottomed or cast iron fry pan on medium-high heat to pre-heat. Wait until pan begins to smoke slightly then add oil to coat bottom of pan. Add scallops carefully, leaving at least $1/2$ inch (1.2 cm) space between them. Sear scallops in multiple batches if you must, to avoid overcrowding. After 1 minute, loosen scallops from bottom of pan using tongs or a spatula. Continue to cook over high heat for 1 minute. Turn scallops over and sear for an additional 2 minutes.

To serve, spoon some sauce onto each plate and arrange 3 scallops on top. Lightly sprinkle with sea salt and black pepper.

Scallops are the adductor muscle of a shellfish, available in different sizes. Seafood items that weigh less than a pound each are numbered by pieces per pound. For example, 16/20 shrimp means there are 16 to 20 shrimp for each pound. The smaller the number, the larger the shrimp or scallop and the higher the price.

Mussels in Beer
with Mustard Seed, Onion and Herbs

WINE OR CREAM are the most common simmering agents for mussels, but beer adds a great flavor, and goes so well with mustard seed that we often prefer it to the classics. A dark beer such as a stout or porter adds an intense sweet flavor and aroma, where a wheat or Oktoberfest beer adds a light and grainy taste. Both are appropriate – the choice is yours.

Be sure to have a loaf of rye or whole wheat bread handy for dipping into the sauce.
Serves 6

2 Tbsp.	olive oil	30 mL
1	onion, julienned	
2	cloves garlic, sliced	2
6 lbs.	fresh mussels, cleaned and debearded	2.75 kg
3 cups	beer	720 mL
1	lemon, sliced	1
1½ Tbsp.	dry mustard seed	22.5 mL
2	sprigs fresh thyme	2
2	sprigs fresh tarragon	2
2	sprigs fresh mint	2
2	sprigs fresh marjoram	2
1½ tsp.	salt	7.5 mL
	pepper	

In a large stockpot, heat oil over medium-high heat. Add onion and sauté for 5 minutes until tender. Add garlic and sauté 1 minute more. Add mussels and sauté for 3 minutes, stirring occasionally and gently. Pour in beer, add lemon, mustard seed and herbs and cover pot.

Steam mussels until they open, for 5 to 10 minutes (depending on size). Season with salt and pepper and remove herb stems before serving.

The only issue in serving mussels is to make sure that they are tightly closed and cleaned right before they go into the pot. Any mussel that is cracked or remains open when tapped should be discarded; double-check immediately before cooking. Keep them on ice in the fridge until ready to use, not under water. To debeard mussels, simply pull off the seaweed-like string that sticks out from the shell (not all mussels have them).

Mussels are delicious, nutritious and affordable seafood that produce a great broth from their cooking liquid. Don't be shy – try any flavors you like:
- *tomato, fennel and white wine*
- *bacon, garlic and red wine*
- *leeks, spinach and cream*

61

Chilled Poached Salmon
on Sweet Pepper Sauces

POACHING SALMON does not have to be a difficult process. By using an instant-read thermometer, available at most kitchen stores, you can immediately tell when the salmon is done. This prevents overcooking your portions of fish to the point that they crumble as you remove them from the poaching liquid.

Poaching salmon in a fish stock builds a beautiful flavor, but you can also use vegetable stock or water, with the addition of an onion, a rib of celery, and an extra cup of white wine to create a flavorful poaching liquid.

Serves 6

Poached Salmon

4 cups	Fish Stock (page 21)	1 L
1 cup	white wine	240 mL
2	lemons, sliced	2
2	sprigs fresh thyme	2
	salt and pepper	
6	6-oz. (170-g) portions of salmon fillet, pinbones removed	6

Sweet Pepper Sauces

2	red bell peppers, seeded	2
2	yellow bell peppers, seeded	2
1	small Yukon Gold potato, peeled and diced	1
1	onion, diced	1
2	cloves garlic, sliced	2
1 cup	white wine	240 mL
1 cup	water	240 mL
2	sprigs fresh thyme	2
	salt and pepper	

Preheat oven to 275°F (135°C). In a flat-bottomed roasting pan or pot (sides of pan need to be at least 4 inches (10 cm) high, simmer stock, wine, lemons, thyme, salt and pepper. Place salmon pieces in the liquid, leaving some space between them for even cooking, and remove pan from heat.

Cover pan with its lid or foil and place it in oven. Cook for 15 to 20 minutes, checking temperature after 15 minutes. The internal temperature of the salmon should be 145°F (62°C) and the flesh should feel firm. Remember, the salmon will continue to cook after it is removed from the oven. Using a slotted spoon or spatula, gently remove each piece from the liquid, and place on paper towels or a rack to drain. Chill for at least 4 hours before serving.

To prepare sauces, place red and yellow peppers in separate small pots (or sauces can be made one at a time) with half of each of the remaining ingredients. Simmer for 20 minutes. Remove sprigs of thyme and purée each sauce separately with a hand blender or in a food processor. Strain, season to taste and chill.

To serve, spoon each sauce onto the plate for a side-by-side contrast, or create your own pattern with dots and lines. Place a salmon piece on each plate.

The best part of planning to serve a chilled dish is that most of the work can be done ahead of time so that before serving all you have to do is assemble. If you like salmon rare, remove it sooner than 20 minutes. If you want your salmon fully cooked, then leave it for the full cooking time. Eat food that makes you happy.

At the restaurant we buy fresh fillets from Heritage Salmon, a producer of certified Fundy salmon. Farmed Atlantic salmon is consistent in quality and price and offers exceptional flavor.

63

Pan-Roasted Rosemary Salmon
on Gamay Beetroot Butter

THIS DISH IS BEST cooked in smaller portions, so a single serving can be used as an appetizer, or two pieces for an entrée. The attractively colored sauce can be made from freshly prepared beets, although it is a great way to use up leftovers.

Salmon portions can be cut from a side of salmon, or ask the fish department of your grocery store to portion it for you.
Serves 6

12	sprigs fresh rosemary	12
12	3-oz. (85-gm) portions of Atlantic salmon fillet, skin on	12
	salt and pepper	
4 Tbsp.	vegetable oil	60 mL

Gamay Beetroot Butter

2	beets, cooked in water with a splash of vinegar added, peeled and diced	2
1	shallot, minced	1
¹/₂ cup	Gamay wine	120 mL
	juice of 1 lemon	
¹/₂ cup	unsalted butter, cut into pieces and chilled	120 mL
	salt and pepper	

To prepare salmon, begin by removing some of the rosemary leaves from the stems by running your fingers against the grain, thus pulling away leaves that can be saved for later use. Stick a rosemary stem through the side of each portion of salmon. Lightly season with salt and pepper. Heat a heavy-bottomed fry pan over medium-high heat and pour in oil (use half the oil if cooking salmon in 2 batches). Place salmon in pan skin-side down and cook for 7 to 9 minutes, until salmon becomes light pink. As it cooks and the rosemary warms, the scent will transfer to the salmon. Loosen the fillets using a spatula. The skin will have become crispy and delicious.

To make beetroot butter, place beets, shallot, wine and lemon juice in a small saucepot and simmer until liquid is reduced by $3/4$. Add butter a piece at a time, stirring constantly, until it is fully incorporated. Season with salt and pepper.

To serve, spoon a little sauce on the plate and arrange salmon fillets on top. Sprinkle a little lemon juice over the salmon and enjoy.

❧ *The earthy, rich sweetness of beets provides a great complement to salmon with its crispy skin and pink inside. Try this dish as a second appetizer with Cave Spring Gamay before the meat course of a dinner party.*

Facing page: Blue Cheese and Apple Salad with Boston Lettuce and Walnuts (page 53)

Following page: Beet, Grapefruit and Parmesan Salad (page 54)

Grilled Tuna with Tapenade
and Gazpacho Sauce

Tuna takes well to stronger flavors such as olives and highly seasoned gazpacho.
Serves 6

Tapenade

1 cup	kalamata olives, pitted	240 mL
2 tsp.	capers	10 mL
$\frac{1}{2}$ tsp.	anchovy paste	2.5 mL
1	clove garlic, chopped	1
	juice of 1 lemon	
4 Tbsp.	olive oil	60 mL
	pepper	

Gazpacho Sauce

3	ripe tomatoes, chopped	3
	or	
1	14-oz. (398-mL) can tomatoes	1
2	green onions, chopped	2
$\frac{1}{2}$	red bell pepper, seeded	$\frac{1}{2}$
$\frac{1}{4}$	English cucumber, chopped	$\frac{1}{4}$
1	clove garlic	1
1 Tbsp.	white wine vinegar	15 mL
	juice of 1 lime	
2 Tbsp.	olive oil	30 mL
2 Tbsp.	fresh basil chiffonade	30 mL
2 Tbsp.	finely chopped fresh chives	30 mL
1 Tbsp.	finely chopped fresh coriander	15 mL
	salt and pepper	
6	5-oz. (140-g) portions of fresh tuna loin	6
	olive oil	
	salt and pepper	

To prepare tapenade, place olives, capers, anchovy paste, garlic, lemon juice, olive oil and pepper in a food processor and blend until smooth. Set aside.

For gazpacho sauce, purée tomatoes, green onions, red pepper, cucumber, garlic, vinegar, lime juice and olive oil in a food processor until evenly blended. Stir in herbs and season to taste. Chill until ready to serve.

Preheat grill to high heat. Lightly brush tuna with oil and season with salt and pepper. Grill tuna evenly on all sides. Grilling time depends on thickness of portions and desired temperature. At the restaurant, we serve the tuna rare on a pool of gazpacho, with a dollop of tapenade on the tuna.

❧ *Ask for impeccably fresh, deep red steaks with no black parts or odor. Allow tuna to sit with the oil at room temperature before grilling, to take the chill off. Treat good tuna like beef fillet, charring the outside and leaving it rare in the middle.*

Facing page: Chilled Poached Salmon on Sweet Pepper Sauces (page 62)

Preceding page: Sea Scallops on Apricot Butter Sauce (page 60) with Lacy Potato Cakes (page 99)

Fried Monkfish and Ragout
of Thyme, Figs and Coriander

THIS DISH IS COMPOSED of several strong flavors that harmonize well. If fresh figs are not available, dried can be substituted.
Serves 6

Ragout

1	onion, julienned	1
1	rib celery, diced	1
2 Tbsp.	olive oil	30 mL
1 cup	white wine	240 mL
1 cup	Fish Stock (page 21)	240 mL
	zest and juice of 1 lemon	
2 tsp.	fresh thyme	10 mL
9	fresh or 6 dried figs, quartered	9
3 Tbsp.	chopped fresh coriander	45 mL
1/4 cup	unsalted butter (optional)	60 mL
	salt and pepper	

Monkfish

4 Tbsp.	vegetable oil	60 mL
1/2 cup	cornmeal	120 mL
1/2 cup	flour	120 mL
	salt and pepper	
6	8-oz. (225-g) fillets of cleaned monkfish	6

To prepare ragout, sauté onion and celery in olive oil over medium heat in a large sauté pan until translucent, about 5 minutes.

Add wine, stock, lemon zest and juice, and thyme and simmer for 20 minutes, allowing some of the liquid to evaporate. If you are using dried figs, add them at this point to re-hydrate. If you are using fresh figs, add them immediately before serving along with coriander and butter. Season to taste.

To fry monkfish, heat a heavy-bottomed fry pan with vegetable oil over medium-high heat. Blend cornmeal and flour and season with salt and pepper. Dredge fish in flour mixture, shaking off any excess. Place fish carefully into fry pan and cook for 5 minutes. Using a spatula, turn fish and cook on other side, another 5 minutes. To serve, spoon ragout over fish.

Monkfish is sometimes called "poor man's lobster," but I don't think it really resembles lobster. It has a great flavor and texture of its own and can be fried, grilled or braised. Just trim off any of the gray skin left on the fillets and cut them into medallions, or little steaks 1 1/2 inches (4 cm) thick. When the fish is done, it will feel slightly firm and some of its juices will have congealed on the outside.

Rob Fracchioni, one of our sous chefs, brings in fresh figs from his mother's garden and we treat them like gold. He arrives with the little treats packed into egg crates with paper towels on top – it's really quite a sight.

Roasted Halibut
with Corn Chardonnay Butter

THE SWEETNESS OF FRESH CORN matches well with the delicate flavor of halibut. Using a Chardonnay without a lot of oak for the sauce will bring out the character of this dish. If fresh corn is not available, use good-quality frozen corn and add about 2 Tbsp. (30 mL) water or stock to the sauce in place of the sugary liquid that is produced when corn kernels are removed.

Serves 6

6	6-oz. (170-g) fresh halibut fillets	6
2 Tbsp.	olive oil, for brushing	30 mL
	salt and pepper	
1½ tsp.	finely chopped fresh thyme	7.5 mL
	juice of 1 lemon	
1 cup	Chardonnay wine	240 mL
1	shallot, minced	1
1 cup	fresh corn, removed from the cob, liquid reserved	240 mL
½ cup	unsalted butter, cut into pieces and chilled	120 mL
	salt and pepper	

Preheat oven to 375°F (190°C). Lightly oil a baking sheet or line with parchment paper. Place halibut on pan and lightly brush fish with oil, then sprinkle it with salt, pepper and ½ the thyme. Roast for 15 to 20 minutes, until fish layers just pull away when touched with a fork. Sprinkle fish with lemon juice immediately before serving.

Meanwhile, prepare sauce by placing wine, shallot and reserved juice from corn cobs into a small pan. Simmer until liquid is reduced by ½. Add corn and thyme and bring up to a simmer again. Reduce heat to low and add cold butter a piece at a time, stirring until all of the butter is incorporated. Season with salt and pepper and serve over halibut.

Summer season ensures that corn comes in so sweet and juicy that you can eat it right off the cob. At the restaurant, we cut the kernels off and make a broth from the cobs, which is then reduced to use in this sauce—a sort of rich, boozy, creamed corn. Just for the "halibut," you can avoid butter by puréeing the reduction.

Pan-Roasted Pickerel
with Rhubarb Leek Butter

ALTHOUGH LEMON is the most common accent to fish, we find that rhubarb provides the required acidity with a delicate fruit flavor. Save the tops of the leeks in this recipe to flavor a stock!

Serves 6

6	6-oz. (170-g) portions of pickerel (equivalent to 3 fillets, halved)	6
	salt and pepper	
1½ Tbsp.	unsalted butter	22.5 mL
1½ Tbsp.	vegetable oil	22.5 mL

Rhubarb Leek Butter

1 Tbsp.	unsalted butter	15 mL
2	leeks, white and light green part only, sliced and well washed	2
1 cup	fresh rhubarb, diced	240 mL
½ cup	white wine	120 mL
¼ cup	sugar	60 mL
½ cup	unsalted butter	120 mL
1	sprig fresh thyme, finely chopped	1
	salt and pepper	

Preheat oven to 375°F (190°C). Season fish with salt and pepper. To roast pickerel, heat a heavy-bottomed fry pan (with ovenproof handle) on medium-high heat. Add butter and oil and wait until butter begins to foam. Carefully place fish flesh-side down in pan, and cook until it is lightly browned, about 3 or 4 minutes. Turn fish over and place pan, uncovered, in oven. Roast for 8 to 10 minutes, until flesh can be easily separated with a fork.

Meanwhile, heat a small saucepan over medium heat. Add 1 Tbsp. (15 mL) butter and sauté leeks until tender, around 5 minutes. Add rhubarb, white wine and sugar and simmer until liquid is reduced by half. Add remaining ½ cup (120 mL) butter a piece at a time until all of it is incorporated. Add thyme and season with salt and pepper.

As a child, fishing "on the point" at the lake in Saskatchewan meant going after pickerel for its succulent sweet flesh. You can cook the fish in this recipe entirely on the stovetop, but using the partial oven method results in a more evenly cooked fish and frees up your time to finish sauces and other dishes.

Seafood Hot Pot
with Saffron Aïoli

USE YOUR FAVORITE fish and seafood.
Similar to a classic bouillabaisse, this meal is
served with a highly seasoned mayonnaise
on the side.

Serves 6

2 Tbsp.	vegetable oil	30 mL
1	small onion, julienned	1
1	rib celery, diced	1
1	carrot, diced	1
2	cloves garlic, minced	2
1 cup	white wine	240 mL
3 cups	fish or shellfish stock (page 21 or 22)	720 mL
1 lb.	fresh mussels, debearded	455 g
4 oz.	fresh salmon, diced	113 g
4 oz.	fresh halibut, diced	113 g
4 oz.	tiger shrimp, deveined	113 g
4 oz.	bay scallops	113 g
1 tsp.	fresh thyme, chopped	5 mL
1	tomato, diced	1
1	potato, cooked, peeled and diced	1
½ cup	corn or peas	120 mL
2 Tbsp.	fresh basil chiffonade	30 mL
1 Tbsp.	fresh dill, chopped	15 mL
	salt and pepper	

Saffron Aïoli

¾ cup	mayonnaise (see page 24)	180 mL
2	cloves garlic, minced	2
pinch	saffron	pinch
	juice of 1 lemon	

In a large saucepot, heat oil and sauté onion,
celery and carrot until tender, about 5 minutes.
Add garlic and sauté 1 minute more. Flush
vegetables with wine and stock and bring to a
simmer. First add mussels, cover pot and simmer for 2 minutes. Then add fish, cover and
simmer 2 minutes more. Finally, add shrimp,
scallops, thyme, tomato, potato and corn (or
peas) and simmer, covered, for another 2 to
3 minutes or until mussels open. Season with
basil, dill, salt and pepper immediately
before serving.

To prepare aïoli, stir together mayonnaise
and garlic. Combine the saffron and lemon
juice and let them sit a few minutes to allow
flavor and color to be drawn out. Then stir
juice into mayonnaise.

To serve, ladle hot pot into wide-mouthed
soup bowls and spoon a dollop of aïoli directly
on top or onto a piece of toasted French bread
on the side, to dip into the broth.

*Use whatever fish and shellfish are avail-
able. Delicate items need less cooking time
and should be added near the end.*

69

Trout Baked in Parchment
with Mint and Riesling

THE PRESENTATION of this dish is spectacular, and the joy in it is that the assembly can be done ahead of time. As mint is one of the first herbs to appear in the spring (and it grows like a weed), this entrée is suited to the season and would be appropriately paired with Asparagus in Lemon Butter.

Parchment paper is silicone-treated paper that can tolerate high oven temperatures. Size your sheets approximately 14 inches (36 cm) by 20 inches (50 cm) for each portion of trout. You will need 6 sheets of parchment paper for 6 servings of trout.

Serves 6

6	8-oz. (225-g) trout fillets, pinbones removed	6
3	shallots, peeled and thinly sliced	3
12	sprigs fresh mint	12
6	slices lemon	6
³/₄ cup	Riesling wine	180 mL
	salt and pepper	
6 Tbsp.	unsalted butter	90 mL

Preheat oven to 375°F (190°C). Fold each sheet of parchment paper in half, press a crease on the fold, and open. Place a trout fillet flesh-side up on lower half of parchment. Sprinkle fish with half a sliced shallot and place two sprigs of mint on top. Arrange 2 lemon slices over mint and sprinkle with 2 Tbsp. (30 mL) of Riesling. Season trout with salt and pepper and dot with 1 Tbsp. (15 mL) butter. The wine, butter and juices from the fish will work together to make a sauce as the fish cooks.

To prepare the trout for baking, fold over the top of the parchment so that the fish is covered and edges of the paper meet. At one folded side of the paper, begin by making a

small fold upwards, about 1½ inches (4 cm). Using your finger to hold the first fold, make another fold to overlap half of the first one, thus holding it in place. Continue making such overlapping folds, working around the fillet in a semi-circle, until you reach the opposite folded side of the paper. At this point, give the paper a good twist around with your fingers. This will create a sealed package in which the trout can bake.

Place parchment parcels on an ungreased baking sheet and bake for 12 to 15 minutes. You will know they are ready when the steam from the fish inflates the parcels.

To serve, place entire parcel on a plate and either tear carefully with your fingers (beware of steam) or cut open with scissors.

Cooking food inside a parchment envelope is a great way to use natural flavors as part of the steaming process. The delicious aroma of herbs is released at the dinner table as your guests tear open their "package." The use of butter or oil can be avoided completely if you choose, as the wine and lemon (and even moisture in the fish) produce the steam for cooking. The same technique can be used for mushrooms, chicken, or shrimp and scallops. The key is in the folding: just make sure that each fold seals the previous one.

Cave Spring Dry Riesling works nicely with lightly flavored freshwater fish, with the wine's hints of citrus fruit, skate-blade acidity and clean finish. When you cook richer dishes like scallops or halibut, reach for more full-bodied white wines like Off-Dry Riesling or Chardonnay Bench.

71

POULTRY

Poultry is one of the most frequently cooked meats in the home kitchen because it is affordable and versatile. The following recipes are some of our most popular from Inn on the Twenty's menu history and, although very simple to prepare, they require quality raw ingredients above all.

We used to have the apprentices do written reports on different ingredients and then present them to the whole kitchen staff. A young cook named Chris had chicken as his topic and in his haste misquoted King Louis of France proclaiming that "on Sundays he hoped every pheasant in the country would have a chicken in the pot."

A great childhood memory of mine was Mom pan-frying a grouse my brother Mark had shot. I remember the meat being rich and nutty tasting, and much to my 12-year-old delight, I found a piece of lead shot in my portion. What a rugged adventure! After I recounted the tale to Mark recently, he said the prairie chicken (as it is called in Saskatchewan) was nasty and tough. Hey Mark—get off my memory cloud!

We hope that our recipes, such as the Chicken on the Grill with Cider Vinegar and Herbs, or Chicken Breast Filled with Brie, Basil and Sundried Tomato, can be wonderful memory builders in your home.

Whole Roast Chicken
with Celeriac, Onion and Lemon

THERE ARE FEW AROMAS better than that of a chicken roasting in the oven. Add to that the scent of onion and lemon and you have a feast for the senses. Try this with a generous helping of White Cheddar Grits.

Serves 6

2	onions, julienned	2
1	rib celery, diced	1
1	5-lb. (2.25-kg) chicken	1
2	lemons, sliced	2
2	sprigs fresh thyme	2
6–8	fresh sage leaves	6–8
	salt and pepper	
2 Tbsp.	butter, melted (optional)	30 mL
1	celeriac (celery root), peeled and diced	1

Lemon Chardonnay Sauce

1½ cups	Dark Chicken Stock (page 19)	360 mL
¼ cup	Chardonnay	60 mL
1	lemon, zested and juiced	1
¼ cup	green onions, chopped	60 mL
1 Tbsp.	unsalted butter	15 mL
	salt and pepper	

Preheat oven to 350°F (175°C). Place ½ the onion and celery in the bottom of a roasting pan and lay chicken on top. Place remaining onion and 1 of the sliced lemons, along with the sprigs of thyme and 3 or 4 sage leaves, inside chicken cavity. Using your hands, gently lift the skin of the chicken to separate it from the breast meat, being careful not to tear it. Slide 2 or 3 lemon slices underneath the skin and arrange remaining sage leaves over the lemon slices. The lemon scent will permeate the chicken as it roasts. Season the chicken with salt and pepper and, if desired, baste lightly with melted butter.

Roast uncovered in the oven for 75 to 90 minutes, basting frequently, until juices run clear. Thirty minutes before finishing, add celeriac and toss into basting juices.

To make the sauce, simmer chicken stock with wine, lemon juice and zest and green onions and reduce by ½. Add to this the juices from the roasting pan and butter. Season to taste.

Once chicken has been removed from roasting pan, spoon out celeriac with onions and celery and serve vegetables tossed together with sauce on the side.

Celeriac is the underground portion of a celery plant grown not for the stalks we are accustomed to using, but for the bulb itself. When cooked it has a tremendous taste with a smooth, almost custard-like texture. I think this simple meal is the perfect match for Cave Spring Chardonnay Reserve.

Stuffed Chicken Breast with Brie,
Basil and Sundried Tomato

THIS DISH IS GREAT to prepare at home, since it creates its own sauce. When you slice into the chicken, the juices of the meat mixed with the melted Brie make a wonderful combination. It has been a popular feature at Inn on the Twenty for many years.

Skinless breast can be used with success, but the crispiness of browned skin is a delight. *Serves 6*

6	chicken breasts, boneless with skin	6
6 oz.	Brie cheese, sliced	170 g
12	fresh basil leaves	12
12	sundried tomatoes, rehydrated	12
	salt and pepper	

Preheat oven to 350°F (175°C). Using a sharp knife, slice lengthwise across each chicken breast. Inside each slit, place a slice of Brie, 2 leaves of basil and 2 sundried tomatoes. Place chicken in a roasting pan or on a baking sheet and season with salt and pepper.

Roast chicken for 25 minutes, until juices run clear. Don't worry if some cheese runs out onto the pan; simply spoon it over the chicken when serving.

Filling a breast of chicken adds appeal to the dish and prevents the meat from drying out. Like great classics, Kiev or Cordon Bleu, this dish makes eyes roll because it is so good yet so simple.

Best results come from choosing good-quality chicken. "Low temperature scald" refers to the part of the plucking process that leaves the skin more yellow and thus more juicy. "Air chilled" means the bird has not been cooled in water, which tends to wash out flavor. Whether you call it free range, organic or kosher, rely on your butcher to sell you a quality bird. Regardless of label, the proof is always in the taste.

75

Pan-Roasted Chicken Breasts
with Caramelized Shallots

SHALLOTS CAN BE SLOW-ROASTED in the oven while other tasks around the kitchen are being done. Pan-roasting the chicken creates that delicious (if a little sinful) crispy skin.
Serves 6

4 Tbsp.	vegetable oil or butter	60 mL
1 lb.	shallots, peeled	455 g
½ cup	white wine	120 mL
2 Tbsp.	balsamic vinegar	30 mL
½ cup	light or dark chicken stock (page 18 or 19)	120 mL
6	boneless chicken breasts, skin on	6
	salt and pepper	

Preheat oven to 350°F (175°C). For caramelized shallots, melt ½ of the butter or oil in an ovenproof pan and add shallots. Toss shallots well to coat and place pan, uncovered, in the oven. Roast for ½ hour, tossing shallots once.

Add white wine and vinegar and continue roasting until tender, about 45 minutes more. Remove from oven and place pan on stove over medium heat. Add chicken stock, reduce by ½ and season to taste before serving.

To pan-roast chicken, heat a heavy-bottomed ovenproof pan over medium-high heat until it just begins to smoke. Add remaining oil or butter and heat until the mixture begins to foam. Place seasoned chicken skin-side down in pan and sear for 3 minutes. Place pan in oven for 15 to 20 minutes to roast and then return it to stove burner. Turn chicken and finish cooking, about 5 minutes more.

To serve, slice chicken breasts into 2 pieces on an angle and spoon caramelized shallots and sauce over top.

Shallots look like small onions with a dark skin and they have a wonderfully sharp, strong flavor. Buy ones that are firm and dry and have no green sprouts. The roasted shallot is soft, sweet and rich with a big flavor that is like the sticky onions in a pot roast.

76

Cider Vinegar Grilled Chicken

THE FLAVOR OF A CHARCOAL GRILL adds so much to this dish, but a gas grill will work just fine. Adding the vinegar to the chicken while it's on the grill creates a fair bit of smoke, and the aroma will probably draw the attention of your neighbors.

Serves 6

6	chicken breasts, on the bone	6
1/3 cup	vegetable oil	80 mL
1/2 cup	chopped green onions	120 mL
1/4 cup	chopped fresh basil	60 mL
1/4 cup	chopped fresh parsley	60 mL
2 Tbsp.	chopped fresh thyme	30 mL
2 Tbsp.	chopped fresh rosemary	30 mL
	salt and pepper	
1/2 cup	cider vinegar	120 mL

Preheat grill to medium-high heat. Toss chicken breasts with vegetable oil, green onion, herbs and black pepper and marinate in the refrigerator for 1 to 4 hours. To grill, season chicken with salt and place breasts skin-side down on grill. Cover and cook for 15 minutes. Turn chicken and cook 10 to 15 minutes more (depending on the heat of your grill).

As chicken breasts start taking on color, about 2/3 through the cooking process, begin sprinkling them with vinegar. Continue to do so periodically until all the vinegar has been used.

Vinegar means "sour wine" and is very important in cooking, as it commonly is used to balance the taste of a dish against salt or richness. Cider vinegar goes very nicely with chicken, but you may very well use balsamic, white wine, red wine, basic white or raspberry vinegar — any of these will work. Take advantage of the summer season and make your own flavored vinegars by steeping raspberry, basil, thyme or mint in good-quality wine vinegar.

Cornish Game Hen
Stuffed with Leek Cornbread

CORNISH HENS ARE a perfect single serving size with a great space for stuffing. By baking the key flavor component into the cornbread, little is needed to attain a great flavor.

Serves 6

6	slices bacon	6
1	recipe Leek Cornbread (page 164)	1
2 tsp.	finely chopped fresh thyme	10 mL
1	rib celery, diced	1
1	egg, lightly beaten	1
1/3 cup	chicken stock (page 18)	80 mL
	salt and pepper	
6	Cornish game hens, about 1 1/2 lbs. (680 g) each	6

Preheat oven to 350°F (175°C). Fry bacon until it's crisp and crumble it onto a plate. In a bowl, crumble up cornbread and add thyme, celery, egg, stock, salt and pepper and bacon. Toss until evenly moistened. Distribute stuffing evenly among the cavities of the Cornish hens. Hens do not need to be trussed, but legs can be tied together with butcher's twine, or the cavity can be closed by skewering together the sides of skin over the opening.

Place hens in a roasting pan, leaving an inch or two (2.5 to 5 cm) between the birds, and roast for 1 hour to 1 hour and 15 minutes, until juices run clear and internal temperature reads 185°F (85°C). Untie legs or remove skewer before serving.

Quail in Molasses Glaze

THIS IS A DISH to send you to your butcher for help. While the availability of quail is increasing, they are somewhat challenging to work with because of their dainty size. Ask your butcher if he can "debone" your quail, that is, remove the breast bones while leaving the leg bones intact.

Serves 6

1	green onion, minced	1
¼ cup	blackstrap molasses	60 mL
¼ cup	apple cider	60 mL
2 tsp.	cider vinegar	10 mL
2 tsp.	sugar	10 mL
	salt and pepper	
6	quail, deboned	6
	vegetable oil	

Preheat grill to medium-high. Combine all ingredients except quail in a small saucepot and simmer for 15 minutes, until a glaze consistency is reached.

To grill quail, lightly season with salt and pepper and brush lightly with a little oil. Place them skin-side down on the grill, spreading quail so the legs and breasts are exposed to the heat. Cook for 5 minutes and turn over. Brush birds generously with glaze. Due to the high sugar content, the glaze will caramelize quickly. After 5 minutes, turn quail again, brush once more with glaze, remove from heat and serve.

One of the first farmers I met in Niagara was Joe Speck, who produces only quail and his birds have been on every one of our menus. He runs a top-notch operation and, being only 10 minutes away, he has made some emergency deliveries when we've run low.

Joe told me of an occasion when he was involved in a Hungarian Folk Dance Festival and, running late, he forgot his shoes so he had to perform in his work boots as part of his costume. Each time he slapped his ankle as part of the dance, a small cloud of feathers was released into the air onstage. As much as I have never wanted to see anyone do the Chicken Dance, I would pay good money to watch Joe in "The Dance of the Seven Quails."

Seared Duck Breast
in Sour Cherry Cabernet Gastrique

THIS HAS BECOME a winter staple dish at Inn on the Twenty. A "gastrique" is a classic French sauce that is not often seen, but tastes great with many meats, including lamb, pork and veal. Unlike so many French sauces that are laden with butter, this sauce is fat free! The intensity of flavor is built through the combination of wine, vinegar and sugar, but is softened by the use of sour cherries.

Serves 6

1½ cups	Cabernet wine	360 mL
1½ cups	red wine vinegar	360 mL
2 cups	sugar	475 mL
1 cup	sour cherries	240 mL
6	duck breasts, boneless, skin on	6
	salt and pepper	

For gastrique sauce, place wine, vinegar, sugar and cherries in a medium saucepot and simmer until sauce is reduced by ⅔ and coats the back of a spoon. The color of the cherries will blanch out at first, but then a deep red color will return as the sauce reduces.

To cook duck breasts, preheat oven to 375°F (190°C). Heat an ovenproof sauté pan over medium-high heat. Place duck breasts skin-side down in pan and season lightly with salt and pepper. Sear breasts for 5 minutes and place entire pan, uncovered, in the oven for 15 to 20 minutes until duck is medium rare to medium, depending upon your taste.

Remove duck from pan and allow it to rest for 5 minutes. Slice breasts thinly against the grain and spoon sauce over to serve.

Unlike chicken or turkey, duck breast does not have to be cooked well done; however, the legs should be braised for a long time, as they can be tough. Treat duck breast like a beef steak and leave a pink center to keep it from drying out. Cook duck skin-side down to render the fat and provide a crisp outside. Serve with cheddar mashed potatoes for "cheese and quackers."

Duck goes nicely with many tender fruits. If cherries are not available, try plums, red or black currants or blackberries.

Facing page: Seared Duck Breast in Sour Cherry Cabernet Gastrique (page 80) on Sweet Potato and Celery Root Gratin (page 98)

Following page: Stuffed Chicken Breast with Brie, Basil and Sundried Tomato (page 75) with Rosemary Olive Oil Roast Potatoes (page 100) and Root Vegetable Confit (page 120)

Holiday Turkey
with Barley, Pine Nut and Dried Cherry Stuffing

THIS FESTIVE RECIPE provides an alternative to the traditional bread stuffing.

Serves 12

Stuffing

2 cups	dried pearl barley, rinsed	475 mL
6 cups	light or dark chicken stock (page 18 or 19)	1.5 L
2 Tbsp.	unsalted butter	30 mL
1	onion, diced	1
½ cup	pine nuts	120 mL
½ cup	dried cherries	120 mL
1½ Tbsp.	chopped fresh thyme	22.5 mL
1 Tbsp.	chopped fresh sage	15 mL
½ cup	white wine	120 mL
	zest of 2 lemons	
4 Tbsp.	unsalted butter, melted	60 mL
	salt and pepper	

Turkey

1	16-lb. (6.75-kg) turkey	1
2	onions, diced	2
4	ribs celery, diced	4
3	carrots, diced	3
2	sprigs fresh thyme	2
	salt and pepper	

To prepare stuffing, cook barley in chicken stock until tender, approximately 40 minutes. Drain. In a sauté pan, melt butter and sauté onion until tender, about 5 minutes. Toss barley and onion together with pine nuts, cherries, herbs, wine, zest, melted butter and salt and pepper. Fill turkey cavity with stuffing (remaining filling can be baked in a casserole dish). Turkey legs can be tied together with butcher's twine to secure stuffing, or cavity can be skewered.

Preheat oven to 325°F (165°C). In a large roasting pan, place onion, celery, carrot and thyme at the bottom. Place turkey on top and season with salt and pepper. Roast, covered, for 1 hour. Remove cover and roast for 3 to 4 hours, basting frequently, until internal temperature (test between the leg and the breast) registers 185°F (85°C). Remove turkey from oven, take out stuffing, and allow turkey to rest for 15 minutes before carving.

Order your holiday turkey fresh from your butcher rather than using a frozen one. If you do use frozen, defrost it slowly in the refrigerator for two days. You don't want dry turkey, but do ensure that it is thoroughly cooked to 185°F (85°C).

Facing page: Holiday Turkey with Barley, Pine Nut and Dried Cherry Stuffing (this page) and Whole Baked Ham in Thyme Honey Glaze (page 86)

Preceding page: Rack of Lamb in Mustard Crust (page 93) with Garlic-Smashed Yukon Golds (page 102)

MEAT

Steaks, chops, roasts, stew, medallions and cutlets are ordered every day at the restaurant. We have many customers who prefer fish, chicken and vegetarian dishes, but meat still dominates the Canadian palate. In the past several years, we've seen more high-end steakhouses open using more top-quality beef than ever before, and customers demand the very best products. Consult your butcher for advice, keeping in mind that "lesser" cuts can be made delicious by long, slow braising while expensive tenderloin or New York steaks just need a quick turn on the grill or in the fry pan.

Canadian pork is tops in the world and, besides being a great value, it is tremendously versatile. I would love to think that a great retirement project for me would be to travel around to those BBQ rib contests with a big roaster and cook the best pork ribs ever. That would be my RRPSP (Registered Retirement Pig Smoking Plan).

Sauté of Pork Tenderloin
with Apples, Onion and Mustard

WITH ITS AUTUMN flavors, this dish begs to be consumed with Oktoberfest beer!
Serves 6

3	12-oz. (340-g) pork tenderloins	3
2 Tbsp.	vegetable oil	30 mL
1½	onions, julienned	1½
1	rib celery, diced	1
1½	Mutsu apple, peeled and diced	1½
2 Tbsp.	coarse grain mustard	30 mL
1½ tsp.	finely chopped fresh thyme	7.5 mL
¼ cup	apple cider	60 mL
½ cup	chicken stock (page 18)	120 mL
	salt and pepper	
1½ Tbsp.	unsalted butter	22.5 mL

Slice pork medallions about ½ inch (1.2 cm) thick and julienne to create strips. In a large sauté pan, heat oil over medium-high and add pork. Sauté pork until slightly browned and remove from pan.

Add onion and celery to the pan and sauté until tender, about 5 minutes. Return pork to pan with apple, mustard, thyme, cider and stock. Simmer until pork is cooked through and apples are tender, about 5 minutes. Season to taste and stir in butter, to thicken sauce slightly. Serve over egg noodles or spaetzle.

 Pork tenderloin is extremely versatile and takes very little time to cook, grilled whole, roasted in medallions or pan-fried in slivers.

Roast Pork Rack with Maple Beer

IF RACK OF PORK is not available, substitute a boneless, center-cut pork loin roast.
Serves 8

2	shallots, minced	2
1 cup	dark beer	240 mL
½ cup	maple syrup	120 mL
2 tsp.	chopped fresh thyme	10 mL
2 tsp.	Dijon mustard	10 mL
	salt and pepper	
1	6-lb. (2.7-kg) rack of pork	1

To make glaze, simmer shallots, beer, maple syrup, thyme, mustard, salt and pepper for 15 minutes. Preheat oven to 375°F (190°C).

Place rack on a roasting pan and season with salt and pepper. Score in a crosswise direction just to, but not through, the surface of the meat. Roast uncovered for 1 hour, beginning to baste with glaze after ½ hour. Baste frequently until internal temperature of pork reaches 140°F (62°C). Remove rack from oven and let rest 10 minutes before carving.

Pork "Capicollo" Steak
Braised in Tomato with Olives

THE "ZING" OF OLIVES lightens the richness of this braised dish. Shoulder steaks can be used instead of capicollo for the same flavorful effect.

Serves 6

4	slices bacon, diced	4
6	8-oz. (225-g) capicollo steaks	6
	or	
3	1-lb. (455-g) pork shoulder steaks, cut in half	3
1	onion, diced	1
2	ribs celery, diced	2
2	carrots, diced	2
2	cloves garlic, minced	2
1 cup	white wine	240 mL
1	28-oz. (796-mL) can diced tomatoes	1
2 tsp.	chopped fresh thyme	10 mL
2	bay leaves	2
½ cup	kalamata olives, pitted	120 mL
	salt and pepper	

Preheat oven to 325°F (165°C). In a large ovenproof pot, fry bacon until crisp. Remove bacon and leave some fat. Over medium-high heat, sear capicollo steaks in bacon fat until brown and remove.

Reduce heat to medium and sauté onion, celery and carrot until tender, about 5 minutes. Add garlic and sauté 1 minute more. Add white wine, tomatoes, herbs and olives and bring to a simmer. Stir pork and bacon into sauce and season to taste. Cover and place in oven for 2 to 2½ hours, until pork pulls apart easily with a fork.

Serve in a bowl with crusty bread or with potatoes or buttered noodles.

While we generally think of capicollo as a rubbery little cold cut, it actually refers to the neck muscle from which the cured meat was originally made. Since it's a less tender cut of meat, a long slow braise is the cooking method that will render the meat tender and enrich the sauce with natural juices.

This is a non-fussy cold weather dish that tastes even better reheated the next day for lunch (or in a sandwich during a late night cheesy space movie fest). Need a little spice in your life? Add anchovy purée and chili peppers.

Whole Baked Ham
in Thyme Honey Glaze with Horseradish Beets

SPECTACULAR HOT from the oven or chilled and served whole the next day, holiday ham is a great treat. The herb-infused honey glaze has a great aroma and complements the ham wonderfully.
Serves 12

1	12-lb. (5.4-kg) bone-in ham	1

Glaze

½ cup	chicken stock (page 18)	120 mL
½ cup	white wine	120 mL
½ cup	honey	120 mL
1	bunch fresh thyme	1
	salt and pepper	

Horseradish Beets

3	beets, cooked, peeled and diced	3
1 Tbsp.	white wine vinegar	15 mL
3 Tbsp.	grated horseradish	45 mL
	salt	

Preheat oven to 325°F (165°C). Score surface of ham to allow for expansion, and bake for 3 to 4 hours.

Meanwhile, place all glaze ingredients in a saucepot and simmer for 20 minutes, until mixture thickens somewhat. Strain out thyme.

After 2 hours of baking, begin glazing ham, and baste frequently until it is done.

Using a hand blender or food processor, blend together beets, vinegar, horseradish and salt. Serve at room temperature as a relish with the ham.

Every Christmas we have a big party on the 23rd, to wish our friends well and count our blessings. This ham is a trademark, placed on our hutch, and is more user-friendly than a plate of decorated canapés.

"Hmm . . . there's a chunk of meat with a knife and mustard. I think I know what to do . . . yes, yes, that's it! Ha . . . me smart."

Veal Medallions
in Truffled Malted Cream

MALT IS A FANTASTIC FLAVOR to add to mushrooms (and of course so is truffle). At the restaurant, we use malt extract, which is used most commonly in baking, but if you cannot find this regular Ovaltine has the right flavor. Truffle accentuates the intensity. If you are entertaining a larger group, you may want to make the sauce ahead of time and roast the tenderloin whole, then slice it tableside.

Serves 6

2 lbs.	veal tenderloin	900 g
4 Tbsp.	vegetable oil	60 mL
2	shallots, sliced	2
1¼ lbs.	mixed mushrooms, such as crimini, portobello and shiitake	565 g
1	clove garlic, minced	1
1 tsp.	chopped fresh thyme	5 mL
¼ cup	white wine	60 mL
1 tsp.	malt extract	5 mL
	or	
1 Tbsp.	Ovaltine	15 mL
½ cup	beef stock or dark chicken stock (page 20 or 19)	120 mL
1½ cups	whipping cream	360 mL
	salt and pepper	
dash	truffle oil	dash

To prepare veal, slice tenderloin into ¾ inch (2 cm) slices and pound to ¼ inch (.6 cm) between 2 pieces of plastic wrap. Heat a fry pan over medium-high heat with half the vegetable oil. Season veal and pan-fry until cooked, about 8 minutes.

For sauce, heat a large sauté pan with remaining vegetable oil. Sauté shallots for 2 minutes. Add mushrooms and sauté until natural juices are evaporated, about 8 minutes. Add garlic, thyme and white wine. Simmer for 1 minute. Stir in malt extract (or Ovaltine) and add beef stock. Simmer until liquid reduces by half, 6 to 8 minutes. Add cream and bring to a simmer for 3 minutes. Season to taste and add a dash of truffle oil. Spoon over veal to serve.

Elegant as they may be, veal and truffles are not too hard to manage–just don't overcook the meat. You can certainly do without truffle oil and even malt, as the mushroom cream is really the backbone of this dish.

A rich, full-bodied Chardonnay goes nicely with this dish; this is the time for a barrel-fermented oaky monster such as Cave Spring Estate Chardonnay.

Onion-Marinated Striploin Roast
Wrapped in Spinach and Prosciutto

PURÉED ONIONS create one of the most flavorful marinades we have ever made at Inn on the Twenty, and also reduce the need for excessive oil as a conduit for seasonings. The outside layers of spinach and prosciutto make for an elegant presentation.

If you are unsure as to how to clean the striploin of fat, ask your butcher to do it for you.
Serves 12

1	6-lb. (2.7-kg) beef striploin, cleaned of all fat and sinew	1
4	onions	4
4	cloves garlic	4
	salt and black pepper	
1 Tbsp.	chopped fresh thyme	15 mL
³/₄ lb.	thinly sliced prosciutto	340 g
4 cups	loosely packed baby spinach leaves	1 L
2 Tbsp.	vegetable oil	30 mL

Split striploin roast in half lengthwise, to create 2 pieces that are about 3 inches (7.5 cm) wide. In a food processor, blend onion, garlic, salt, pepper and thyme and spoon over beef sections. Cover and chill the striploin for a minimum of 1 hour to as long as overnight.

Preheat oven to 375°F (190°C). Spread a sheet of parchment paper onto the counter. Using ¹/₂ the prosciutto, line parchment with overlapping slices the length of one striploin piece and just over the width of its diameter. Cover prosciutto with ¹/₂ the spinach leaves.

Rub off excess onion mixture from one piece of striploin and season meat with salt and pepper. In a fry pan heated over medium-high heat, sear striploin in oil on all sides until browned. Place beef at one end of paper. Using the paper, roll up striploin with the spinach and prosciutto layers. Twist end of paper to seal and place meat in a roasting pan. Repeat procedure for second piece of striploin.

Roast for 35 to 45 minutes. For medium-rare, the internal temperature will read 130°F (52°C). Let rest for 10 minutes before carving. Unwrap paper and slice striploin into ¹/₂-inch (1.2-cm) pieces.

Don't worry! This is as easy as assembling a jelly roll and the prosciutto flavors the meat and keeps it moist. For a slightly more complex dish, add a layer of herbed cheese, puréed cooked mushrooms, or cooked sausage meat between the spinach and the beef.

You will need a full-bodied red wine to go with this dish, such as the Cave Spring Cabernet Sauvignon.

Parmentier of Beef
with Spicy Sweet Potato Crust

THIS UPSCALE VERSION of shepherd's pie is a popular item on our winter lunch menu. While at the restaurant we serve it baked in individual molds, this dish can be prepared at home in a casserole dish, served "family-style."

Serves 6

Beef Parmentier

2 lbs.	beef sirloin	900 g
1/3 cup	flour	80 mL
4 Tbsp.	vegetable oil	60 mL
1	onion, diced	1
2	parsnips, diced	2
2	cloves garlic, minced	2
1/2 cup	red wine	120 mL
2 tsp.	finely chopped fresh thyme	10 mL
1 1/2 cups	beef stock (page 20)	360 mL
dash	allspice	dash
	salt and pepper	

Sweet Potato Crust

3	sweet potatoes, peeled and diced	3
1	chipotle chili pepper, rehydrated and finely chopped	1
3 Tbsp.	unsalted butter	45 mL
1/2 tsp.	chopped fresh thyme	2.5 mL
	salt and pepper	

To prepare beef, slice sirloin into 1/4-inch (.6-cm) strips, and chop those slices into thin pieces (emincée). Toss the beef in flour and shake off any excess. In a medium pot heated with oil, brown meat thoroughly and remove. Reduce heat to medium, add onion and parsnip and sauté until tender, about 5 minutes. Add garlic and sauté 1 minute more. Add red wine, thyme, stock, allspice and salt and pepper and simmer for 40 minutes, until beef is tender and sauce has thickened.

Meanwhile, to prepare sweet potatoes, boil diced potatoes in salted water until soft. Drain well and mash using an electric mixer, adding chili pepper, butter, thyme and salt and pepper.

Preheat oven to 350°F (175°C). To assemble, spoon beef mixture into a casserole dish and smooth sweet potatoes on top with a spatula. Bake, uncovered, for 20 minutes. Let rest 5 minutes before serving.

I ate a version of this dish at a bistro in Paris and the simple, robust and yes, recognizable, taste made me close my eyes and savor the moment.

Assemble this dish a day ahead for convenience (you can make two and freeze one), and bake it while you make a simple green salad or Blue Cheese and Apple Salad. Serve with a slightly chilled Gamay.

Beef Tenderloin Meurette

THIS DISH IS A GOURMAND'S "steak and eggs." A poached egg is served atop a pan-roasted beef fillet that, when cut, spills into the beef reduction to produce a deliciously rich blend.

Serves 6

6	strips bacon, diced	6
1½	onions, julienned	1½
½ lb.	mixed mushrooms, chopped	225 g
½ cup	red wine	120 mL
3 cups	Beef Stock (page 20)	720 mL
3 Tbsp.	unsalted butter	45 mL
6	eggs	6
2 Tbsp.	white vinegar	30 mL
6	6-oz. (170-g) beef tenderloin fillets	6
	salt and pepper	

To prepare sauce, cook bacon until it is crisp in a medium saucepot. Remove bacon, leaving some fat. Sauté onions over medium-low heat, stirring occasionally, until they begin to caramelize, about 25 minutes. After cooking onions for 15 minutes, add mushrooms and sauté. Add red wine and stir to remove flavorful bits from bottom of pan.

Add beef stock and bring to a simmer. Reduce sauce by ⅔, season and stir in butter until incorporated.

To poach eggs, bring a pot of water to simmer and add vinegar. Stir water to create a little whirlpool and crack in egg. Poach egg until white is cooked and yolk is soft, about 5 minutes. Remove egg with a slotted spoon and reserve in a dish of warm water until ready to serve. Repeat with remaining eggs.

Meanwhile, to prepare beef, preheat oven to 400°F (200°C) and heat an ovenproof skillet over medium-high heat with a splash of oil. Season beef fillets with salt and pepper and place in pan. Sear beef on both sides and place entire pan in the oven. If you do not have a pan large enough to fit all 6 fillets with an inch (2.5 cm) of space in between them, sear beef in batches and place them on a lightly oiled baking sheet to roast. Roast until beef is medium-rare: 130°F (52°C). Let rest 5 minutes before serving.

To serve, place a beef fillet on each plate (or a platter) and place a poached egg gently on each. Spoon sauce over each egg and serve.

> ✿ *The success of this dish is in the sauce. Start with good stock and reduce it to concentrate the flavor. For a Sunday lunch treat, use smaller steaks and serve with Sweet Potato and Celery Root Gratin.*

Crusted Beef Fillet
with Blue Cheese and Walnuts

BLUE CHEESE is a popular garnish for beef, and here we have incorporated it into the cooking process. The crust resembles a cobbler topping, and holds in the juices of the beef as it cooks.

Serves 6

4 Tbsp.	vegetable oil	60 mL
6	6-oz. (170-g) beef fillets	6
	salt and pepper	
6 oz.	blue cheese	170 g
1 cup	breadcrumbs	240 mL
$^3/_4$ cup	walnuts, toasted and chopped	180 mL
$^1/_4$ cup	white wine	60 mL
$^1/_2$ tsp.	chopped fresh thyme	2.5 mL
$1^1/_2$	shallots, minced	$1^1/_2$

Preheat oven to 375°F (190°C). To prepare beef, heat oil in a fry pan over medium-high heat. Season beef and sear evenly on both sides. Place beef on a baking sheet or roasting pan.

Combine remaining ingredients in a bowl to make crust. Add a sprinkle of water, if needed, to bind everything together. Using your hands, scoop up crust, pack it slightly and place an equal amount on top of each fillet. Roast fillets in oven for 20 minutes, until medium-rare: internal temperature of 130°F (52°C). Let rest 5 minutes before serving.

If you've been saving a big bottle of Cabernet for a special meal, get the cork out! Rich beef is enhanced by the salty, creamy tang of blue cheese and walnut tannins provide a great bridge to the wine.

The idea of a cobbler-style crust is something with which we have enjoyed experimenting, borrowing from a dessert technique. The topping should be golden brown and crisp on top and moist inside; as it cooks it bastes and flavors the meat. Try the same technique on salmon or halibut, substituting horseradish and butter or sour cream for the blue cheese and walnuts.

Lamb Shanks in Gamay
with Rosemary-Scented White Beans

THIS WAS ON THE FIRST menu at Inn on the Twenty, and has made regular appearances since then. The art of braising turns this tough, but flavorful, cut of meat into a succulent and tasty meal. The rosemary-scented beans add a Provençal accent to the dish.
Serves 6

Lamb Shanks

4 Tbsp.	vegetable oil	60 mL
6	lamb shanks	6
1	onion, diced	1
2	ribs celery, diced	2
2	carrots, diced	2
2	cloves garlic, sliced	2
1 cup	white wine	240 mL
1	28-oz. (796-mL) can diced tomatoes	1
2	sprigs fresh thyme	2
2	bay leaves	2
	salt and pepper	

Rosemary-Scented White Beans

1 cup	dry white beans	240 mL
5 cups	chicken stock (page 18)	1.2 L
1/2	onion	1/2
2	sprigs fresh rosemary	2

Preheat oven to 350°F (175°C). To prepare lamb, heat oil in a large ovenproof pan or saucepot over medium-high heat. Sear lamb until brown on all sides and remove. Add onion, celery and carrot and sauté for 5 minutes, until tender. Add garlic and sauté 1 minute more. Add wine, tomatoes, herbs and salt and pepper and bring to a simmer. Return lamb to pan and cover. Roast lamb in the oven for 2 to 3 hours, until meat begins to pull away from the bone.

To cook beans, rinse and sort through dry beans. Soak them for 1 hour in hot water, then simmer in chicken stock with onion and rosemary until tender, 40 to 50 minutes. Drain excess liquid and season lightly with salt and pepper.

To serve, spoon beans into a bowl or toss directly into sauce, and serve lamb with sauce on top.

This dish is a lamb version of Osso Buco, in which veal shanks are braised in wine and tomato. Lamb shanks can be cooked whole for a single portion.

A classic accompaniment to a rich braised item like this is gremolata, made from equal portions of lemon zest, parsley and fresh garlic. The sharp, intense flavors "lift up" the heavier richness of the meat.

Rack of Lamb in Mustard Crust

AN ELEGANT DINNER ENTRÉE, lamb in mustard crust looks like it takes a great deal of work, but it is relatively simple to prepare. The ideal sauce to serve with this is a reduction of beef stock with red wine and a touch of butter stirred into it.

Serves 6

3	12-oz. (340-g) frenched lamb racks	3
½ cup	Dijon mustard	120 mL
2	shallots, minced	2
2 Tbsp.	chopped fresh rosemary	30 mL
2 Tbsp.	white wine	30 mL
	salt and pepper	

Preheat oven to 375°F (190°C). Place lamb racks in a roasting pan. Combine remaining ingredients and rub generously over lamb. Roast lamb for approximately 25 minutes for medium-rare; an internal temperature of 130°F (52°C). Allow lamb to rest for 5 minutes before carving.

Ask your butcher for enough lamb to suit the number of guests you are hosting. You can coat the lamb a day ahead and leave it in the refrigerator (preferably uncovered) so the mustard dries onto the surface of the meat. Allow the racks to sit on the counter for 15 minutes prior to roasting, just so the center isn't ice cold.

When you present the lamb rack on a plate, place the starch component (such as garlic mashed potatoes) just left of center on the plate. Cut each rack into chops and set the first with the bone resting on the potato with the meat portion at 8 o'clock and bone stretching up and right. Continue to place the chops in a counter-clockwise fashion, showing off the meat and overlapping the bones. Pour a little sauce around the front of the meat and serve.

Venison Chili
with Roasted Garlic Custard Tart

THE ROASTED GARLIC custard tart is a delicious treat that is great on its own with a salad. The venison chili is sweet and rich, without being too heavy.

Serves 6

Venison Chili

2 lbs.	venison hind, diced into ½-inch (1.2-cm) cubes	900 g
4 Tbsp.	flour	60 mL
4 Tbsp.	vegetable oil	60 mL
1	onion, diced	1
2	ribs celery, diced	2
2	carrots, diced	2
2	parsnips, diced	2
3	cloves garlic, minced	3
1 cup	red wine	240 mL
3 Tbsp.	blackstrap molasses	45 mL
1 cup	apple cider	240 mL
1	14-oz. (398-mL) can diced tomatoes	1
1 cup	beef stock (page 20)	240 mL
2 tsp.	chopped fresh thyme	10 mL
1	bay leaf	1
2 Tbsp.	red wine vinegar	30 mL
	salt and pepper	

Roasted Garlic Custard Tarts

1	recipe Brisée Pastry (page 124)	1
1 cup	milk	240 mL
4	egg yolks	4
1 tsp.	sugar	10 mL
¾ tsp.	salt	4 mL
2 Tbsp.	cornstarch	30 mL
1 Tbsp.	roasted garlic	15 mL
1 Tbsp.	unsalted butter	15 mL
¼ cup	whipping cream, whipped	60 mL

To prepare chili, toss venison in flour and shake off excess. Heat oil in a large saucepot over medium-high heat, sear venison until brown and remove. Reduce heat to medium and sauté onion, celery, carrot and parsnip until tender, about 7 minutes. Add garlic and sauté 1 minute more. Add red wine, molasses, cider, tomatoes and stock and bring to a simmer. Add venison, thyme and bay and simmer for 1½ hours, until venison is tender. Before serving, add vinegar and season to taste.

To make custard tarts, roll brisée pastry on a lightly floured surface and line 6 individual tart shells with pastry. Chill for ½ hour. Preheat oven to 375°F (190°C). Blindbake shells for 15 minutes. Remove weights and continue to bake shells for 10 minutes more, until golden brown.

To prepare custard, heat milk to a scald in a small saucepot. Meanwhile, whisk together egg yolks, sugar, salt, cornstarch and garlic. While whisking constantly, gradually add hot milk to egg mixture. Return combined ingredients to pot over medium heat. Whisk custard until it thickens (this will happen quickly) and remove from heat. Whisk in butter and spoon custard into a bowl. Cover custard with plastic wrap touching the surface, to prevent a skin from forming, and chill 2 hours. After custard has chilled, fold in whipped cream.

To serve, spoon custard into tart shells. These can be served as is, or broiled for 30 seconds to brown the top. Serve chili beside tart.

As with our "cobbler" topping for beef fillet, we've adapted another dessert idea to savory cooking. Instead of the custard being sweet and intended for fruit, we've replaced the sugar with roasted garlic and paired it with venison stew.

I tasted something like this, a southwest version, at Star Canyon in Dallas during a cooking competition and we've manipulated the recipe to suit our style. I hate to say it, but a chef once said to me, "My boy, the sooner you realize there are no new ideas, the better off you'll be." New dishes come from so many inspirations: our personal backgrounds, TV, magazines, books, other restaurants and current consumer and health trends. Although I would never downright copy another dish, any kitchen certainly looks to others for motivation and inspiration.

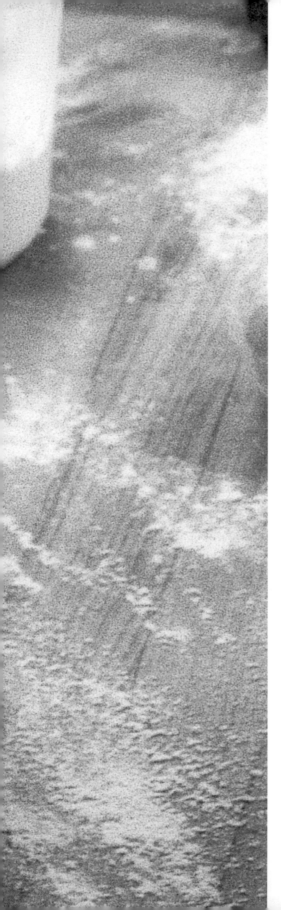

POTATOES,
PASTAS AND OTHER
FILLING THINGS

The recipes included in this chapter are meant
as sides to a main course or, in some cases, a
meal unto themselves. Combining one of these
(without meat) with some of our vegetable
ideas makes a well-rounded vegetarian meal.

As North Americans, we naturally gravi-
tate toward potatoes as a starch on our plate.
While we provide many tasty preparations for
potatoes, a pasta or risotto served either as an
appetizer or as a side dish provides a great
alternative. If you serve such dishes as
appetizers, you don't need a starch at all
on your main course plate.

Sweet Potato and Celery Root Gratin

THE CONTRAST IN FLAVOR and color is very appealing in this dish. Great with roast chicken or pork rack, gratins are easy to prepare if the oven is already heated.
Serves 6 to 8

1½ lbs.	sweet potatoes, peeled	680 g
1	medium celery root, peeled	1
3	shallots, sliced	3
1½ cups	whipping cream	360 mL
1 Tbsp.	chopped fresh thyme	15 mL
	salt and pepper	
1 Tbsp.	unsalted butter	15 mL
1	clove garlic	1
½ cup	grated Romano cheese	120 mL

Preheat oven to 350°F (175°C). Slice sweet potatoes and celery root thinly.

In a small saucepot, heat shallots with cream, thyme and salt and pepper to allow flavors to infuse.

Lightly butter a 12-cup (3-L) baking dish and rub with a clove of garlic. Layer overlapping slices of sweet potato along the bottom of the dish. Ladle a little cream over potato slices and sprinkle with a touch of grated Romano. Follow this with a layer of celery root slices, repeating cream and cheese steps. Continue until all ingredients are in the dish. Pour over any remaining cream and sprinkle with cheese. Press down on the gratin with the flat side of a spatula.

Bake, covered, for 1 hour. Uncover gratin and bake for an additional 20 minutes, to brown top.

Sweet potatoes are not yams! Yams are larger, rounder and waxy looking. This gratin is a more elegant version of scalloped potatoes and smells delicious cooking in the oven. You can substitute chicken stock for the cream for a low-fat version.

Lacy Potato Cakes

THIS RECIPE serves well when you are looking for something with showy presentation. Easy to prepare ahead of time, these crispy potato cakes go nicely with salmon, chicken or pork.

Serves 6

3	large Yukon Gold potatoes, peeled	3
	salt and pepper	
	vegetable oil	

Julienne potatoes into matchstick-size pieces by hand, or by using a mandolin. Immediately sprinkle salt over potatoes to prevent them from discoloring. Season with pepper.

Into a small non-stick sauté pan, pour about $\frac{1}{4}$ inch (.6 cm) vegetable oil and heat over medium heat. Spoon in $\frac{1}{2}$ cup (120 mL) of potatoes and spread evenly in a circle in the pan. Allow potatoes to sizzle and brown until crisp on one side before turning. Turn carefully using a spatula and cook until other side is brown. Remove and allow to drain on a cooling rack. Repeat the process until all potato has been used.

To serve, potato cakes can be warmed in a low-temperature oven and they will remain crispy.

Unlike potato pancakes made from a batter, or roesti made from shredded cooked potato, these potato cakes are very crunchy and make an excellent base for grilled scallops or roasted pork. The starch of this large potato binds the panckes firmly together. Yukon Golds were developed at the University of Guelph, and these yellow-fleshed marvels are seen on menus across North America.

Salt-Roasted Mini Potatoes

ROASTING POTATOES on a bed of salt imparts an even and delicious flavor without using any fat. Don't throw away the salt after cooking. It can be used again for roasting.
Serves 6

| 3 lbs. | mini potatoes, washed | 1.35 kg |
| 2 lbs. | rock salt or pickling salt | 900 kg |

Preheat oven to 350°F (175°C). Spread salt evenly onto a baking sheet. Place potatoes on top of salt and bake for 30 to 45 minutes (depending on size) until tender. There is no need to turn potatoes as they cook; they will absorb salt flavor evenly.

This method cooks and seasons the potato in one effort; try the leftovers in home-fries or potato salad. This is also a great way to do baked potatoes or "creamers" (the smallest of the new potatoes) for filling with sour cream, smoked salmon and caviar.

Rosemary Olive Oil Roast Potatoes

THE DISTINCT FLAVOR of olive oil infused with rosemary creates a great pairing for just about any meat or poultry. Regular olive oil is fine to use, or extra virgin if you wish a more pungent flavor.
Serves 6

3 lbs.	mini potatoes, washed	1.35 kg
6 Tbsp.	olive oil	90 mL
1 Tbsp.	chopped fresh rosemary	15 mL
	salt and pepper	

Preheat oven to 375°F (190°C). Cut potatoes in half. Toss with oil, rosemary, salt and pepper until evenly coated and place on a baking sheet or roasting pan. Roast for 30 to 45 minutes, stirring occasionally.

Extra virgin olive oil is pressed without heat or other means to force extraction. It is best used where its flavor is noticeable: over tomatoes, salad greens or vegetables. Use a decent mid-range olive oil for cooking, especially when flavoring with herbs like rosemary.

Chuck's Potato Salad

THIS GERMAN-STYLE potato salad should be served warm. Delicious with chicken, pork or fish, this potato salad is not limited to the summer season.

Serves 6

4	slices bacon, diced	4
1	onion, diced	1
5	Yukon Gold potatoes, peeled and diced	5
1 tsp.	chopped fresh thyme	5 mL
1 cup	chicken stock (page 18)	240 mL
1/4 cup	whipping cream	60 mL
2 Tbsp.	white vinegar	30 mL
	salt and pepper	

In a sauté pan over medium heat, sauté bacon until crisp and remove. Drain off all but 2 Tbsp. (30 mL) fat and sauté onions until tender, about 5 minutes. Add potatoes and thyme and sauté 2 minutes. Add stock and cream and simmer until potatoes are tender, approximately 20 minutes. Add vinegar and stir in bacon. Season to taste and serve warm.

Chuck Eller is a sous chef at Inn on the Twenty and thoroughly enjoys cooking anything that uses pork, from bacon to rack of pork.

101

Lime-Roasted Sweet Potatoes

THE SIMPLICITY of this accompaniment is enhanced by the delicious flavor. Just a little lime juice adds such a "zing" to sweet potatoes.

Serves 6

3 lbs.	sweet potatoes, peeled and diced	1.35 kg
4 Tbsp.	olive oil	60 mL
2 tsp.	finely chopped fresh thyme	10 mL
	juice of 4 limes	
	salt and pepper	

Preheat oven to 350°F (175°C). Toss all ingredients together to mix well, then place on a baking sheet. Roast in the oven for 25 to 35 minutes, stirring occasionally, until fork-tender.

This method is great with Cider Vinegar Grilled Chicken or Grilled Tuna with Tapenade and Gazpacho Sauce. If you're cooking outdoors, wrap the potatoes in foil and do them on the BBQ rather than turning on the oven.

Garlic-Smashed Yukon Golds

THE RESURGENCE of mashed potatoes as a fine food is not ignored here. Quite often, our guests will ask for a second helping of this ideal comfort food on the side. The mashed potatoes can be prepared with or without the peels on; the choice is yours.

Serves 6

3 lbs.	Yukon Gold potatoes, peeled (optional) and diced	1.35 kg
4 Tbsp.	unsalted butter	60 mL
3	cloves garlic, minced	3
⅔ cup	milk	160 mL
	salt and pepper	

Boil potatoes, starting with cold salted water, until fork-tender. Drain thoroughly and return to pot.

Melt butter in a small sauté pan over low heat and add garlic to cook the flavor into the butter. Add milk just to warm. Using an electric beater or a hand masher, mash potatoes while adding butter and milk. Season to taste. Be careful not to overbeat, or a gluey product will result.

Who would believe that mashed potatoes would be as fashionable as we've seen over the past years? I think it has to do with the "been there, done that" approach to food that North Americans have adopted. We've traveled and experimented and have come back to things that taste great and are made without too much fuss.

Smashed potatoes make a great base for piling on everything from a grilled beefsteak to pan-fried shrimp or even the starch component of a vegetarian meal. If any remain, they can be fried into potato cakes or they can be used as the topping on our Parmentier of Beef, in place of the sweet potato.

102

Baked Gnocchi
with Bacon and Blue Cheese

THIS IS A DISH for those whose vocabulary does not include the word "diet." The big flavors in this pasta come from the big use of cream!

Serves 6

1½ lbs	fresh or frozen gnocchi	680 g
2 Tbsp.	olive oil	30 mL
6	strips bacon, diced	6
3	shallots, sliced	3
1 cup	white wine	240 mL
3 cups	whipping cream	720 mL
2 tsp.	chopped fresh thyme	10 mL
6 oz.	blue cheese	170 g
	salt and pepper	

Preheat oven to 375°F (190°C). Cook gnocchi in boiling salted water, drain well, toss lightly with olive oil and reserve.

In a sauté pan over medium heat, fry bacon until crispy and set aside. Drain off all but 1 Tbsp. (15 mL) fat and sauté shallots until tender, about 3 minutes.

Add white wine and reduce liquid by ½. Add cream and thyme and bring to a simmer. Crumble in blue cheese, and return bacon to pan and season to taste. Remove sauce from heat.

Place gnocchi in an ovenproof baking dish and pour sauce over pasta. Bake for 15 to 20 minutes, until sauce bubbles and begins to brown.

103

This dish can be prepped ahead of time and then baked before dinner. It makes a great course on its own between appetizer and main. If you feel adventurous, there are many excellent recipes for making gnocchi from scratch, but there are also some good-quality frozen or premade products on the market.

When cooking dried pasta noodles, generally allow ¼ lb. (125 g) per person and 2 cups (475 mL) of water for cooking each portion. Cook your pasta until tender but still with a resilient bite to it; the best way to test the doneness is to taste it. Pasta should be seasoned either with olive oil or a little juice from the pan before being plated and topped with the sauce.

Linguini with Pepper and Spinach
in Chardonnay Garlic Broth

THIS IS A VEGETARIAN dish that uses wine and roasted garlic to create a very flavorful base. The vibrant colors are appealing from ingredients available in every season.

Serves 6

1½ lbs.	fresh linguini	680 g
	or	
1 lb.	dry linguini	455 g
5 Tbsp.	extra virgin olive oil	75 mL
3	shallots, sliced	3
½	head fennel, thinly sliced	½
4	roasted peppers, peeled and julienned (page 25)	4
1½ Tbsp.	roasted garlic	22.5 mL
1 cup	Chardonnay wine	240 mL
1 tsp.	chopped fresh thyme	5 mL
	salt and pepper	
2 Tbsp.	fresh basil chiffonade	30 mL
2 cups	loosely packed spinach	475 mL

Cook linguini in boiling salted water, drain and reserve. In a large sauté pan, heat 3 Tbsp. (45 mL), olive oil and sauté shallots for 2 minutes. Add fennel and sauté until tender, about 5 minutes. Add roasted peppers, garlic, wine and thyme and bring to a simmer for 3 minutes. Season to taste and add remaining olive oil. Immediately before tossing over linguini, add basil and spinach.

Acini di Pepe
with Eggplant, Tomato and Romano

BECAUSE OF ITS ROUND tiny pearl shape, *acini di pepe* means peppercorn in Italian. Due to its size, this pasta is appropriately cooked "risotto style," adding a little liquid at a time. Please feel free to substitute any small pasta, such as orzo.

Serves 6

4 Tbsp.	olive oil	60 mL
½	onion, diced	½
1 lb.	acini di pepe	455 g
½ cup	white wine	120 mL
4½ cups	Vegetable Stock (page 25)	1050 mL
2	cloves garlic, minced	2
1	small eggplant, diced	1
3	ripe tomatoes, diced	3
	or	
1	14-oz. (398-mL) can diced tomatoes	1
½ tsp.	chopped fresh thyme	2.5 mL
3 Tbsp.	fresh basil chiffonade	45 mL
	salt and pepper	
⅔ cup	grated Romano cheese	160 mL

Heat a medium heavy-bottomed pot over medium heat. Add 2 Tbsp. (30 mL) olive oil and sauté onion until translucent, about 5 minutes. Add dry pasta and stir for 3 minutes. Add white wine and stir until absorbed and then reduce heat to medium-low. Add stock, 1 cup (240 mL) at a time, until each measure is absorbed, stirring regularly, until all liquid is used and acini is cooked through.

Meanwhile, in a large sauté pan over medium-high heat, add remaining oil and sauté garlic and eggplant until cooked, about 7 minutes. Add this to the acini once it is almost cooked. Add tomatoes, thyme and basil and stir until tomato has warmed and is tender, about 5 minutes. Season to taste and stir in cheese immediately before serving.

This dish has that "casserole" appeal that makes it able to stand up on its own as a meal, but is also great as a middle course or as an accompaniment to fish or meat.

Cut this recipe in half to make a tasty appetizer course.

105

Fettucine with Sautéed Beef Tender Tips
and Snow Peas in Horseradish Cream

BEEF AND HORSERADISH are a natural pair and make sense together in a pasta. Although beef tender tips are from the most tender cut, a thinly sliced portion of sirloin or even eye of round can be used instead.

Serves 6

1½ lbs.	fresh fettucine	680 g
	or	
1 lb.	dry fettucine	455g
3 Tbsp.	vegetable oil	45 mL
2 lbs.	beef tender tips, cut into 1-inch (2.5-cm) cubes	900 g
1	leek, washed and sliced (light part only)	1
½ cup	beef stock (page 20)	120 mL
2 cups	whipping cream	475 mL
1 tsp.	chopped fresh thyme	5 mL
2 Tbsp.	horseradish	30 mL
½ lb.	snow peas	225 g
	salt and pepper	
2 Tbsp.	chopped fresh chives	30 mL

Cook fettucine in boiling salted water, drain and reserve.

Heat a large sauté pan over medium-high heat. Add oil and beef and sauté until brown. Remove and reserve. Sauté leek until tender, about 5 minutes. Return beef with stock to the pan and reduce liquid by ½. Add cream, thyme and horseradish and simmer 3 minutes. Add snow peas and simmer 3 minutes more. Season with salt and pepper and toss in chives. Serve over fettucine.

Asparagus Risotto
with Mint and Goat Cheese

THIS VEGETARIAN-FRIENDLY dish has all the characteristics of spring flavors. The goat cheese ties together the asparagus and mint smoothly, creating a surprisingly light combination. Remember, the flavor of fresh mint dissipates quickly, so add it immediately before serving.

Serves 6

2 Tbsp.	vegetable oil	30 mL
1	onion, diced	1
1	rib celery, diced	1
1½ cups	arborio rice	360 mL
½ cup	white wine	120 mL
5 cups	Vegetable Stock (page 23)	1.2 L
1 lb.	asparagus, cut into 1½-inch (4-cm) lengths	455 g
1 tsp.	chopped fresh thyme	5 mL
⅔ cup	goat cheese	160 mL
	salt and pepper	
4 Tbsp.	fresh mint chiffonade	60 mL
2 Tbsp.	chives	30 mL

In a large saucepot over medium heat, sauté onion and celery in oil until tender, about 5 minutes. Add rice and sauté 3 minutes more. Add white wine and stir until liquid is absorbed. Flood rice with stock, 1 cup at a time, stirring frequently until all liquid is absorbed.

Before adding last portion of stock, add asparagus and thyme. Stir in goat cheese and season to taste. Before serving, stir in mint and chives.

We get our asparagus locally and from near Lake Erie from Frank, who travels there 2 or 3 times a week to a farm he knows. In the winter, he makes the same drive for Belgian endive, and never fails to deliver a "groaner" of a joke with his produce.

Frank claims you can actually watch the asparagus grow; in June, a full crop is harvested each day. When they're super fresh, it isn't necessary to peel them, but if you snap the bottom off and fibre comes with the end, it would be best to peel the bottom half of the spear with a vegetable peeler.

107

Spring Pea Risotto
with Sautéed Prawns

AT INN ON THE TWENTY, we use jumbo prawns for this dish. They are slightly sweeter than shrimp, with almost a lobster texture to them. Large tiger shrimp are certainly a delicious substitution if prawns are not available.
Serves 6

4 Tbsp.	vegetable oil	60 mL
1	onion, diced	1
1½ cups	arborio rice	360 mL
½ cup	white wine	120 mL
5 cups	Shellfish Stock (page 22)	1.2 L
1½ cups	peas	360 mL
	zest and juice of 1 lemon	
1 tsp.	chopped fresh thyme	5 mL
1¼ lbs.	prawns	565 gm
2 tsp.	chopped fresh mint	10 mL
1 Tbsp.	fresh basil chiffonade	15 mL
1½ Tbsp.	unsalted butter	22.5 mL
⅓ cup	whipping cream (optional)	80 mL
	salt and pepper	

Heat 2 Tbsp. (30 mL) oil over medium heat in a large saucepot and sauté onion until tender, about 5 minutes. Add rice and sauté 3 minutes more. Flood rice with white wine and stir until all liquid is absorbed. Add stock, 1 cup (240 mL) at a time, stirring very frequently, until risotto is cooked. Before adding last portion of stock, add peas, lemon juice and zest and thyme.

Meanwhile, sauté prawns over high heat in remaining oil until they are pale pink in color.

To finish risotto, add mint and basil and stir in butter and cream (if using). Season to taste.

To serve, spoon risotto into large bowls and arrange prawns on top.

> *The rice should be cooked until it still has a firm center, so the liquid component gives the dish a built-in sauce.*

108

Chicken, Pear and Mushroom Risotto
with Asiago

THE ADDITION OF PEAR to this risotto truly adds a marvelous twist. To serve this dish as an appetizer, simply cut the proportions in half.

Serves 6

4 Tbsp.	vegetable oil	60 mL
1	onion, diced	1
2	cloves garlic, minced	2
1½ cups	arborio rice	360 mL
½ cup	white wine	120 mL
5 cups	chicken stock (page 18)	1.2 L
6	boneless, skinless chicken breasts, diced	6
¾ lb.	mixed mushrooms, diced	340 g
1 Tbsp.	fresh thyme, chopped	15 mL
2	Bartlett or Bosc pears, diced	2
	salt and pepper	
1½ Tbsp.	unsalted butter	22.5 mL
1 cup	Asiago cheese, grated	240 mL

In a large saucepot, heat 2 Tbsp. (30 mL) oil and sauté onion over medium heat until tender, about 5 minutes. Add garlic and rice and sauté 3 minutes more. Flood the rice with white wine and stir until all liquid has been incorporated. Add stock, 1 cup (240 mL) at a time, stirring regularly, until each portion of stock is absorbed.

Meanwhile, in a large sauté pan, heat remaining oil and sauté chicken over medium-high heat until browned and cooked through. Remove from pan. Sauté mushrooms with thyme until cooked. Add chicken and mushrooms to risotto just before it is done. Add pear and season to taste. Immediately before serving, add butter and cheese and stir into risotto until melted.

Learning to cook risotto opens up a new chapter in your personal cookbook. The method is the same, whether it's a plain risotto or mixed with seafood. Use whatever is in season in your neighborhood for a standalone meal or as an accompaniment to a meat or fish course.

A straightforward white wine like the Cave Spring Chardonnay Musque shows off non-oaked, full fruit which complements the pear flavor in this dish.

Pumpkin Risotto
with Sage and Walnuts

TASTY ON ITS OWN or as an accompaniment to an entrée, this vegetarian dish evokes autumn. The aroma of sage and pumpkin is heightened with the addition of a touch of apple cider, another autumn necessity. Don't worry if the diced pumpkin breaks down a little during the cooking process; it adds a creaminess to the risotto without adding cream.

Serves 6

2 Tbsp.	vegetable oil	30 mL
1	onion, diced	1
1½ cups	arborio rice	360 mL
½ cup	white wine	120 mL
1 cup	apple cider	240 mL
4 cups	Vegetable Stock (page 23)	1 L
3 cups	diced pumpkin	720 mL
2 Tbsp.	chopped fresh sage	30 mL
1 tsp.	chopped fresh thyme	5 mL
¾ cup	walnut pieces, lightly toasted	180 mL
	salt and pepper	
1 Tbsp.	olive oil	15 mL
½ cup	Romano cheese, grated	120 mL

In a large saucepot, heat oil over medium heat and sauté onion until tender, about 5 minutes. Add rice and sauté for 3 minutes more. Flood rice with white wine and stir until it is completely absorbed. Add cider and stock, 1 cup (240 mL) at a time, stirring regularly, until each portion of stock is absorbed. Add pumpkin, sage and thyme after cider and allow to cook while risotto is absorbing remaining liquid. Depending on the moisture content of the pumpkin, you may have to add a little more or less liquid.

Before serving, stir in walnuts and season to taste. Add olive oil and Romano immediately before serving.

Pumpkin—it's what's for dinner! The pumpkin serves many purposes other than pie. (Who came up with that one anyway?) It makes delicious soup (serve it in hollowed-out mini pumpkins), vegetable, stuffing, or part of a pasta course. Use a large pumpkin to serve a giant batch of steamed mussels or lamb ragout to a crowd.

Lemon Barley "Risotto"
with Leek and Rosemary

SINCE RISOTTO REFERS to the style of cooking, we have applied this technique to another grain: barley. The flavor of this dish would match well with roast chicken or pork, and can also become vegetarian by using vegetable stock in place of chicken stock. Rinsing the barley before cooking ensures you will have a clean taste and texture, not muddy and sticky.

Serves 6

2	leeks, sliced and washed	2
1	rib celery, diced	1
2 Tbsp.	vegetable oil	30 mL
1½ cups	pearl barley	360 mL
½ cup	white wine	120 mL
6 cups	chicken stock (page 18)	1.5 L
2 Tbsp.	chopped fresh rosemary	30 mL
	zest and juice of 2 lemons	
	salt and pepper	
1½ Tbsp.	unsalted butter	22.5 mL
⅓ cup	Romano cheese, grated	80 mL

Sauté leek and celery in oil in a large saucepot over medium heat until tender, about 5 minutes. Rinse barley until water runs clear and drain well. Add barley to pot and sauté for 3 minutes. Flood barley with wine and stir until liquid is incorporated. Add stock, 1 cup (240 mL) at a time, stirring frequently, until all liquid is absorbed. Before adding final portion of liquid, add rosemary and lemon zest and juice. Season to taste. Immediately before serving, stir in butter and cheese until melted.

Corn and Coriander Spoonbread

CORIANDER GIVES THIS a zing that is a great match with barbequed foods.
Serves 6

2 Tbsp.	vegetable oil	30 mL
1	onion diced	1
4 cups	fresh corn kernels	1 L
4	egg yolks	4
1	whole egg	1
1 cup	milk	240 mL
1 cup	half-and-half cream	240 mL
	salt and pepper	
1 tsp.	chopped fresh thyme	5 mL
1½ Tbsp.	chopped fresh coriander	22.5 mL
	zest of 1 lemon	
2 Tbsp.	cornmeal	30 mL

Preheat oven to 350°F (175°C). Heat oil in a large sauté pan, and sauté onion until tender, about 5 minutes. Add corn and sauté until just cooked, about 4 minutes. Remove from heat and allow to cool.

Whisk together egg yolks, whole egg, milk and cream. Add remaining ingredients and whisk well. Stir in corn and pour batter into a greased baking dish. Place dish into a larger pan and place in oven. Pour boiling water into larger pan to reach halfway up the baking dish and bake for 1 hour.

When Anna makes this dish, I watch people's eyes light up as they bite; the flavor is so sweet and true.

White Cheddar Grits

GRITS ARE THE North American version of polenta. The larger grain goes well with dishes like lemon-roasted chicken.
Serves 6

1 cup	regular grits (not instant)	240 mL
2⅓ cups	water	560 mL
2 Tbsp.	unsalted butter	30 mL
1 cup	grated white cheddar	240 mL
	salt and pepper	
2	green onions, chopped	2

Bring lightly salted water to a boil and whisk in grits. Reduce heat to medium and simmer, covered, for 15 minutes, until water is absorbed.

Stir in butter and cheese until melted and adjust seasoning to taste. Stir in green onions before serving.

Once you make grits, you'll return often for a change from rice or potatoes as a starch for meat, poultry or fish dishes.

Citrus Herbed Wheat Berries
with Spring Vegetables

WHEAT BERRIES may also be sold under the name wheat kernels.

Serves 6

1½ cups	wheat berries	360 mL
1	leek, sliced and washed well	1
1	rib celery, diced	1
4 Tbsp.	olive oil	60 mL
1	red bell pepper, diced	1
¾ cup	peas	180 mL
½ lb.	asparagus, cut into 1½-inch (4-cm) segments	225 g
	zest and juice of 1 lemon	
	zest and juice of 1 orange	
1	green onion, chopped	1
1 tsp.	chopped fresh mint	5 mL
2 Tbsp.	fresh basil chiffonade	30 mL
1 Tbsp.	fresh chervil	15 mL

Cook wheat berries in boiling unsalted water until tender, about 40 minutes. Drain well.

In a large sauté pan over medium heat, sauté leek and celery in 2 Tbsp. (30 mL) olive oil until tender. Add bell pepper, peas and asparagus and sauté until just cooked. Reduce heat to low and add wheat berries. Stir until warm. Add remaining ingredients and toss well.

Served warm, room temperature or chilled, the flavor of this dish improves as it marinates in its vinaigrette.

113

Lovage Flan

THE CLASSIC FLAN is a custard. It's great with roast turkey, quail or chicken and you can try your favorite herb in place of lovage.

Serves 6

3	egg yolks	3
2	whole eggs	2
2 cups	half-and-half cream	475 mL
1	shallot, minced	1
2 tsp.	finely chopped lovage	10 mL
	salt and pepper	

Preheat oven to 325°F (165°C). Whisk together all ingredients and pour into 6 greased 4-oz. (120-mL) ramekins. Place ramekins in a large pan and place in oven. Pour boiling water into pan to reach halfway up ramekins and bake for 25 minutes, until flans soufflé slightly and are set.

To serve, run a knife around the outside of the flan to loosen edges, then turn ramekin onto a plate and lift away.

VEGETABLES

Driving through Niagara in warm weather allows you to "take a reading" of the local farm production simply by checking over any of the farmgate stands that dot the countryside. Many are based on an honor system that allows you to shop and leave your money in a tin box. One sign above a box says, "Careful what you do, God is watching." What a security system! We are lucky to have so many excellent farmers within a few minutes' drive of Jordan and we even have a custom growing plan with some of them.

Choose your own vegetables as they come into season, preferably from sources close to you. We've always felt that "Fresher is better, and closer is fresher." The ultimate compliment to pay a vegetable is to prepare it so that it tastes like the name implies; in other words, a carrot should taste like a carrot, not like sesame oil.

Asparagus in Lemon Butter

"SHOCKING" GREEN VEGETABLES in an ice water bath after blanching ensures that they will keep their vibrant color. The vegetables can then be rewarmed in a pan to serve.
Serves 6

1½ lbs.	fresh asparagus, ends trimmed	680 g
½ cup	white wine	120 mL
	juice of 2 lemons	
1	shallot, minced	1
5 Tbsp.	unsalted butter	75 mL
	salt and pepper	

Bring 8 cups (2 L) of salted water to a boil and add asparagus. Cook until just tender, about 3 minutes, drain and immediately place in a bowl filled with ice water until cold. Drain and reserve until ready to use.

To make lemon butter, reduce white wine and lemon juice with shallot until only 2 Tbsp. (30 mL) of liquid remain. Stir in 4 Tbsp. (60 mL) of butter until incorporated, season to taste and remove from heat. Melt remaining butter in a sauté pan and heat asparagus until just warm (be careful not to overcook). Arrange on a platter or individual plates and spoon lemon butter over spears.

When spring hits we can hardly wait for the first asparagus to appear. I like to eat enough spears in the month of June to get so tired of them that I don't buy the imports out of season. Don't cover green vegetables with a lid when blanching them, as they will turn brown.

116

Braised Belgian Endive
in Riesling and Grapefruit Peel

THIS IS A SIMPLY PREPARED dish with a surprisingly complex flavor. The taste of grapefruit is refreshing, and makes it an excellent accompaniment to lightly seasoned dishes, such as trout or other mild fish.

Serves 6

4	heads Belgian endive	4
2	shallots, sliced	2
1 cup	Riesling wine	240 mL
1	red grapefruit	1
	salt and pepper	
2 Tbsp.	unsalted butter	30 mL

Preheat oven to 350°F (175°C). Trim bottoms of endive, slice in half lengthwise, and arrange in a baking dish. Sprinkle shallots over endive and pour in Riesling. Peel the grapefruit using a vegetable peeler to remove skin without taking the pith. Add to the endive along with the juice from the fruit. Season and dot endive with butter.

Cover and bake for 20 to 30 minutes, until endive is tender when tested with a fork.

117

Maple-Glazed White Turnips

TURNIPS MAY GET THEIR NAME since people walk by them at the grocery store and "turn up" their noses at this root vegetable. Unlike a yellow rutabaga, however, white turnips tend to be milder and have a lower sulphuric component. Glazed with maple syrup, they have pleasantly surprised many of our guests at the restaurant.

Serves 6

1½ lbs.	white turnips	680 g
1 Tbsp.	white vinegar	15 mL
½ cup	chicken stock (page 18)	120 mL
½ cup	maple syrup	120 mL
	salt and pepper	
1 Tbsp.	unsalted butter	15 mL

Peel and cut turnips into wedges. Simmer turnips in boiling water with white vinegar until tender, 15 to 20 minutes. Drain.

Reduce chicken stock and maple syrup in a medium saucepot with turnips, until liquid is absorbed and turnips are evenly glazed, about 5 minutes. Season to taste and stir in butter.

❧ *Maple turnips can be finished in the oven with a chicken or beef roast. The sweetness of the maple glaze brings out a spicy quality in the turnips that is not noticeable when they are served with just salt and pepper.*

Quick Braised Cabbage

WE CALL THIS a "hot slaw." It has all the components of a chilled coleslaw, except that serving it warm makes it a wonderful pairing with fish, chicken or pork, especially in cooler weather.

Serves 6

½	onion, julienned	½
4 Tbsp.	vegetable oil	60 mL
2	cloves garlic, minced	2
6 cups	savoy cabbage, thinly sliced	1.5 L
½ cup	white wine	120 mL
	juice of 2 lemons	
2 tsp.	chopped fresh thyme	10 mL
2 tsp.	chopped fresh dill	10 mL
1	Mutsu apple, diced	1
	salt and pepper	

In a large sauté pan over medium-high heat, sauté onion in oil for 5 minutes until tender. Add garlic and sauté 1 minute more. Add cabbage and sauté for 3 minutes, until it warms.

Flood pan with wine and lemon juice and stir occasionally, letting cabbage steam itself, until it begins to soften but does not become soggy. Add herbs and apple, and season to taste.

Cooked cabbage should be one of two things: either quick and crisp, as in this method, or slow-cooked until meltingly tender. There is no in-between.

Eggplant Caponata

THE SIZE THAT YOU CUT your eggplant will determine the character of this dish. If you want a chunky vegetable course to pair with grilled chicken, cut the eggplant and onion to ³/₄-inch (2-cm) pieces. If you wish something that resembles a relish that could be used as an accent for lamb, cut the vegetables into ¹/₄-inch (.6-cm) pieces.

Serves 6

4 Tbsp.	olive oil	60 mL
1	onion, diced	1
2	ribs celery, diced	2
1	small eggplant, diced	1
2	cloves garlic, minced	2
1 tsp.	chopped fresh thyme	5 mL
1¹/₂ Tbsp.	chopped capers	22.5 mL
2 Tbsp.	red wine vinegar	30 mL
1 Tbsp.	sugar	15 mL
	salt and pepper	

Heat a large sauté pan over medium-high heat. Add olive oil and sauté onion and celery until tender, about 5 minutes. Stir in eggplant and sauté until soft. Add garlic, thyme and capers and reduce heat to medium. Add vinegar and sugar and simmer until liquid is absorbed. Season to taste.

Eggplant is definitely a food that needs work put into it. I can't recall biting into a raw eggplant or even hearing of a raw preparation. Its greatest attribute is that it can absorb flavors and carry them well. Don't be afraid to generously season this dish with herbs, capers and vinegar. It is excellent served cold as a salad component or as part of an antipasto platter.

119

Root Vegetable Confit

ONE OF OUR MOST POPULAR vegetable combinations, we pair this with anything from salmon to veal rack. The color is beautiful and the flavor is hearty and refined simultaneously. You must cook the vegetables separately since they take different lengths of time, and the separate cooking keeps colors defined.

Reserve the oil used to cook because it can be used again and will have attained the sweetness of the cooked vegetables.
Serves 6

2	carrots, diced	2
2	parsnips, diced	2
1	celery root, diced	1
½	rutabaga, diced	½
2	large beets, diced	2
2 cups	vegetable oil	475 mL
	salt and pepper	
2 tsp.	chopped fresh thyme	10 mL

Preheat oven to 350°F (175°C). Place each root vegetable in a separate baking dish and pour even amounts of oil over each.

Cover dishes with foil and cook until each vegetable is tender. Celery root takes the shortest amount of time, about 20 minutes, followed by parsnips at about 30 minutes, carrots and rutabaga at about 40 minutes and finally, beets at about 50 minutes. Drain away oil and set vegetables aside until required.

To serve, heat vegetables together, except beets, in a large sauté pan, season to taste and add thyme. Heat beets separately and toss with other vegetables at the last minute.

This cooking method, known as the confit method, always baffles people at first introduction because of the amount of oil used. Think of the old commercial where they fry chicken and drain all the oil off except 1 teaspoon. The whole idea is similar to roasted vegetables because "shallow frying" is considered a dry heat method. When cooking a vegetable, such as carrots, in water you lose flavor, color and nutrients into the water. Using the confit method, the water in the carrots evaporates and thus concentrates that flavor. Your carrots then turn into "supercarrots" with bigger flavor than you might expect.

Five-Bean Ragout

HIGHLY SEASONED, this combination is great with grilled beef or chicken. The beans need to be cooked separately, as they have varied cooking times.

Serves 6

¹⁄₂ cup	navy beans	120 mL
¹⁄₂ cup	black beans	120 mL
¹⁄₂ cup	romano beans	120 mL
¹⁄₂ cup	lima beans	120 mL
¹⁄₂ cup	adzuki beans	120 mL
3 Tbsp.	olive oil	45 mL
2	shallots, minced	2
2	cloves garlic, minced	2
1 tsp.	ground cumin	5 mL
	juice of 2 limes	
1 tsp.	chopped fresh thyme	5 mL
1 Tbsp.	chopped fresh coriander	15 mL
	salt and pepper	

Sort through each variety of bean and soak separately in hot water for 1 hour. Cook each variety separately in unsalted water until tender. The beans take 45 to 60 minutes to cook, except the adzuki beans, which will take 40 minutes since they are smaller. Drain.

Warm olive oil in a large sauté pan. Sauté shallots for 2 minutes, then add garlic. Add beans, cumin and lime juice and stir until warmed. You may have to add a splash of water to prevent beans from sticking. Add thyme and coriander and season to taste.

Blazing Saddles *was not the inspiration for this recipe. Beans take on flavor very nicely and this dish is excellent with grilled steak, chops or chicken eaten outside with salad and wine. Serve in a vinaigrette with tomato, radish and cucumbers as a chilled leftover salad.*

There are many good-quality canned and freeze-dried multi-bean products available on the market. Such selections work very well in this dish, and leave more time for entertaining or relaxing!

DESSERTS

Anna has been Inn on the Twenty's pastry chef since 1997, after making the move from the savory side of the kitchen. In May 1999 we built a stand-alone dedicated pastry shop on the second floor of the restaurant, which churns out all of the breakfast pastries, breads, dessert sauces and sweets. Unlike the à la carte kitchen, which is noisy and hectic, the pastry department is a refuge, with wonderfully rich aromas, quiet concentrated work and soft classical music in the background.

We like simple, homespun, honest desserts, not too sweet and usually including fantastic fruit. Most of the desserts in this chapter capitalize on fruits harvested during their peak season. The fruit tarts we have included are those that have been the most popular at the restaurant. In the summer we run daily features depending on what arrives at our back door that morning.

To satisfy the sweet tooth, we also have provided recipes for some items that would fall into the category of "rich and gooey." Consistent with all of our cooking, top-notch raw ingredients are the key to successful results.

Brisée Pastry

THIS IS THE BASIC French recipe for pie dough. Made with all butter, it must be rolled while cold. If you wish, you can substitute vegetable shortening for half the butter to make a dough that is not as temperature sensitive.

*Makes crust for a 2-crust pie or
6 to 8 individual tarts*

2 cups	all purpose flour	475 mL
½ tsp.	salt	2.5 mL
1 cup	unsalted butter, cut into pieces and chilled	240 mL
3 Tbsp.	ice water	45 mL

Place flour and salt in a mixing bowl or in an electric mixer fitted with the paddle attachment. Cut in cold butter until texture resembles coarse meal. Add ice water and mix until dough just comes together. Shape into a disc, wrap in plastic and chill until needed, at least 1 hour. Dough freezes well.

As your flour and butter mix, the mixture starts to take on a yellow tone from the butter. At this point, the butter has been evenly worked into the flour without being so incorporated that it will not produce a flaky pastry. It is then that you want to add the water.

Sugar Pastry

THIS CRUST IS always tender, no matter how much you work it. Always blindbake it, to produce a firm base for fruit and cream fillings.

*Makes enough for 1 large fluted pan or
6 individual tarts*

2 cups	all purpose flour	475 mL
⅓ cup	sugar	80 mL
1 tsp.	salt	5 mL
1 cup	unsalted butter, cut into pieces and chilled	240 mL
4	egg yolks	4

Combine flour, sugar and salt in a mixing bowl or in an electric mixer fitted with paddle attachment. Cut in cool butter until flour takes on a yellow tone. Add egg yolks and blend until dough is an even texture. Shape into a disc and chill at least 1 hour before using.

Puff Pastry

THERE ARE BASICALLY 2 methods of making puff pastry, each suited to certain uses. The French method is the classic preparation, making a dough of flour and water and working in a block of butter, rolling and folding at least 6 times. The French technique produces a pastry with flawlessly fine layers and is made when even leavening is important, such as in vol-au-vents. The Dutch method, which we have listed below, is much quicker to prepare, leaves less room for error and does not require folding as many times. For the recipes in this book, the Dutch method serves just fine.

Makes pastry for 2 large or 6 to 8 individual tarts

1¾ cups	all purpose flour	420 mL
¾ cup	pastry flour	180 mL
1¼ tsp.	salt	6.2 mL
1½ cups	unsalted butter, cut into pieces and chilled	360 mL
½ Tbsp.	lemon juice	7.5 mL
⅔ cup	ice water	160 mL

Place flours and salt in a mixing bowl or an electric mixer fitted with paddle attachment. Cut cold butter into dry ingredients until it is the texture of coarse meal, with some small pieces of butter still visible (they will get smoothed out when folded). Combine lemon juice and water and add to dough all at once. Mix until dough just comes together. Shape into a flat rectangle, wrap and chill for at least 2 hours before rolling.

Turn dough onto a lightly floured surface and roll lengthwise to create a long rectangle, about ¾ inch (2 cm) thick. Fold both short ends into the center of the rectangle, then fold dough in half where the first 2 folds meet. Chill 1 hour. Roll pastry again lengthwise to same thickness. Fold dough in thirds and chill 1 hour. Repeat process once more, folding in thirds, chilling at least 1 hour before using.

☙ *When baking any pastry dough, make sure it is well chilled before it goes in the oven, for two reasons. First, it allows the glutens in the flour to relax after rolling, to prevent your dough from shrinking as it bakes and second, it chills the butter so it doesn't leach out of the pastry as it bakes. When the butter melts during baking, the steam produced raises the pastry, creating a flaky, tender crust.*

125

Galette Dough

CORNMEAL AND SOUR CREAM add a nice flavor and texture, while the baking powder helps the crust rise a little as it bakes.

Makes 2 medium free-form tarts
or 8 individual galettes

2 cups	all purpose flour	475 mL
1 Tbsp.	sugar	15 mL
1 Tbsp.	cornmeal	15 mL
½ tsp.	baking powder	2.5 mL
½ tsp.	salt	2.5 mL
1 cup	unsalted butter, cut into pieces and chilled	240 mL
2 Tbsp.	sour cream	30 mL
1–2 Tbsp.	ice water	15–30 mL

Combine flour, sugar, cornmeal, baking powder and salt in a bowl or an electric mixer fitted with paddle attachment. Cut in butter until texture resembles coarse meal. Combine sour cream and water and blend in just until dough comes together. Shape into a disc, wrap and chill at least 1 hour before using.

🌹 *A galette is a free-form tart, so the dough must keep its shape as it bakes and not allow fruit juices to leak through.*

Crepe Batter

THIS FRENCH PANCAKE recipe is very versatile and produces a tender crepe.

Makes 12 large or 24 small crepes

1 cup	all purpose flour	240 mL
1 cup	milk	240 mL
¼ tsp.	sugar	1.2 mL
dash	salt	dash
2½ Tbsp.	unsalted butter, melted	37.5 mL
2	eggs	2

Whisk together all ingredients until smooth. To make crepes, heat a crepe pan or Teflon-coated pan over medium heat and grease lightly. Spoon a little crepe batter into pan and swirl around, creating an even thin layer. Allow to cook until top of crepe loses its shine, about 3 minutes. Turn crepe and cook 30 seconds more. Repeat process, being certain not to stack crepes on top of each other until cool, or they will stick.

Strudel Dough

UNLIKE SO MANY dough recipes, where overmixing is carefully avoided, this recipe requires that the dough be heavily kneaded to develop the glutens in the flour. This kneading will produce a dough that can be easily stretched without any tearing. Use an electric mixer for this dough; kneading by hand would be sticky and take forever.

Makes dough for 2 strudels

1¼ cups	warm water	300 mL
⅓ cup	unsalted butter, melted	80 mL
½ cup + 2 Tbsp.	sugar	150 mL
4 cups	bread flour	950 mL
½ tsp.	salt	2.5 mL
dash	vanilla extract (optional)	dash

Place all ingredients in the bowl of an electric mixer fitted with paddle attachment. Mix for 2 minutes on low speed and then increase to medium speed. Knead dough for 10 to 12 minutes, until dough takes on a stringy appearance. Wrap and let rest at room temperature for at least 1 hour before using.

Strudel dough can be made ahead of time and chilled until ready. Bring dough to room temperature before stretching.

My Great Aunt Nan used to pull strudel with me as a girl. To make sure the two of us were stretching the dough thin enough, Nan would hide a secret note underneath the dough. Once the strudel was stretched across the table, I could read the message, "I love you" right through the dough!

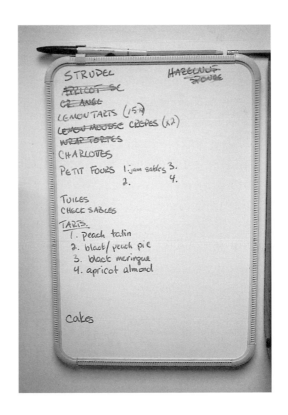

Genoise Sponge Cake

GENOISE IS THE MOST basic of cake recipes. Its light texture makes it versatile for many recipes.

Makes one 9-inch (22-cm) cake

⅓ cup	unsalted butter, room temperature	80 mL
¾ cup + 2 Tbsp.	sugar	210 mL
1 tsp.	vanilla extract	5 mL
4	egg yolks	4
6	egg whites	6
½ tsp.	salt	2.5 mL
1½ cups	all purpose flour	360 mL

Preheat oven to 350°F (175°C). Line the bottom of a 9-inch (22-cm) springform pan with parchment paper (do not butter bottom or sides of pan).

In a bowl or mixer, cream butter with ½ cup (120 mL) of sugar until smooth and pale. Add egg yolks one at a time, beating until each is incorporated, then beat in vanilla.

In a separate bowl, whip egg whites with salt until foamy. Gradually add remaining sugar to whites and whip until soft peaks form.

Using a spatula, gently fold ⅓ of the whites into butter mixture. Add remaining whites and fold gently until just incorporated. Sift in flour and fold, being careful, as the flour tends to sink to the bottom.

Scrape batter into pan and bake for 25 to 30 minutes, until cake springs back in the center when touched. Cool completely before removing from pan.

> *Egg whites will only whip well if the bowl is clean and completely oil-free. To be certain of this, simply wipe the bowl with a paper towel dampened with white vinegar.*
>
> *To change a plain genoise into a nut cake, replace half the flour with your favorite ground nut, such as walnut, almond, hazelnut, or even pistachio.*

Facing page (counterclockwise from top left): Basic Biscuits (page 166), Buttermilk Muffins (page 167), Pecan Sticky Buns (page 165), Quick Breakfast Bread (page 168), Granola (page 170), Palmiers (page 169), Walnut Bread (page 160), Sourdough Bread (page 158), Sunflower Bread (page 156)

Following page (counterclockwise from top left): Lemon Tart (page 138), Raspberry Rhubarb Custard Tart (page 137), Blueberry Minted Custard Tart (page 140), Plum Galette (page 136)

Pastry Cream

PASTRY CREAM is not difficult to make; just be careful when the custard goes onto the stove—the cornstarch sets quickly.

Makes cream for 1 large tart or 6 small tarts

1 cup	milk	240 mL
½	vanilla bean	½
	or	
1 tsp.	vanilla extract	5 mL
4	egg yolks	4
¼ cup	sugar	60 mL
2 Tbsp.	cornstarch	30 mL
1 Tbsp.	unsalted butter	15 mL
⅓ cup	whipping cream	80 mL

Place milk and scraped seeds from vanilla bean (or vanilla extract) in a stainless steel saucepot over medium heat.

In a mixing bowl, whisk together egg yolks, sugar and cornstarch. When milk comes to a simmer, slowly whisk milk into egg mixture, a little at a time, until milk is incorporated. Return mixture to stove, and using a whisk or wooden spoon, cook until custard thickens, about 1 minute. Immediately remove from heat and stir in butter.

Pour custard into a bowl and cover with plastic wrap that directly touches the surface of the custard—this will prevent a skin from developing. Chill. Whip cream until soft peaks form and fold into custard gently.

❧ *Stainless or enamel-glazed pots are best for cooking cream and tomato sauces.*

Chantilly Cream

CHANTILLY CREAM is simply a romantic (and classic) name for whipped cream with a touch of vanilla added.

Makes 2½ cups

1 cup	whipping cream	240 mL
1 Tbsp.	sugar	15 mL
1 tsp.	vanilla extract	5 mL

Whip cream to soft peaks and add sugar and vanilla. Chill until ready to serve.

❧ *When baking, be sure to use pure vanilla extract. The quality will be noticeable. Try adding other flavors to your whipped cream: your favorite liqueur, cinnamon, nutmeg, mint, lemon or orange zest, or lavender.*

Facing page: Lemon Mascarpone and Strawberry Wedding Cake (page 143)

Preceeding page: Peach and Pepper Relish (page 179)

Signature Double Espresso Chocolate Torte

THIS DESSERT has been on our menu since the first day we opened and there would be a rebellion in Jordan if we tried to change it. Have grilled fish and a salad to alleviate any guilt induced by consuming this dessert.

Makes 1 10-inch (25-cm) torte

1 lb. 2 oz.	bittersweet chocolate, cut into pieces	500 g
1⅓ cups	whipping cream	330 mL
¾ cup	unsalted butter	180 mL
6	eggs	6
1 cup	sugar	240 mL
3 Tbsp.	coffee liqueur	45 mL

Preheat oven to 225°F (105°C). Butter a 10-inch springform pan and line bottom and sides with parchment paper.

Place chopped chocolate in a large bowl or in the bowl of an electric mixer fitted with whisk attachment.

Heat cream and butter together just to a simmer. Pour cream mixture over chocolate and let sit 1 minute. Whisk together until smooth.

Whisk together eggs, sugar and liqueur and pour into chocolate mixture. Blend thoroughly, scraping the bottom of the bowl occasionally. Do not whip on high speed. Pour into springform pan and bake for 2 to 2½ hours, until edges are set and center is still slightly soft.

Allow to cool at room temperature. Leaving torte in its pan, refrigerate overnight before cutting.

Your chocolate desserts are only as good as the chocolate you use. The chocolate called for in most baking recipes is couverture chocolate; it has a smooth texture and is made to be melted, unlike chocolate chips, which are made to hold their shape. We use Callebaut chocolate, a Belgian brand available at many specialty food stores. Bittersweet chocolate has slightly less sugar than semi-sweet chocolate, but semi-sweet can be used in this recipe.

Mascarpone Charlotte
with White and Milk Chocolate

THIS IS A "SHOWY DESSERT." A charlotte is a dessert that usually has a sponge cake exterior with a custard or fruit filling. This recipe sits on a sponge cake with a light, almost cheesecake-like filling of two colors swirled on top. At the restaurant, we make individual charlottes, but a large one makes a spectacular presentation at the dinner table.

Makes 1 10-inch (25-cm) charlotte
or 6 individual ones

1	Genoise Sponge Cake (page 128)	1
3½ oz.	white chocolate, chopped	100 g
3½ oz.	milk chocolate, chopped	100 g
3	egg yolks	3
¼ cup	sugar	60 mL
3 Tbsp.	brandy	45 mL
3 Tbsp.	white wine	45 mL
1 cup	mascarpone cheese	240 mL
½ cup	ground nuts (or sliced almonds), lightly toasted	120 mL

Line sides of a 10-inch (25-cm) springform pan with parchment paper or, if using individual ring molds, line each with paper. Slice cake horizontally to create a layer ¾ inch (2 cm) thick. Place cake in bottom of springform, or cut and fit into each mold.

Fill a medium saucepot with 2 inches (5 cm) of water and bring to a simmer. Place white chocolate in a metal bowl and melt over simmering water, stirring constantly. Set aside. Repeat with milk chocolate. Whisk together egg yolks, sugar, brandy and white wine. Whisk over a water bath until mixture leaves a ribbon on itself when whisk is lifted.

Distribute evenly between each bowl of melted chocolate and fold in. Divide mascarpone evenly between two bowls and stir until evenly blended. Fillings will be very glossy and smooth.

Spoon dollops of white chocolate mixture into springform, or fill half of each individual mold. Repeat with milk chocolate mixture, filling in empty spaces. Using a skewer, swirl the two colors together to create a marbled appearance. Chill for at least 4 hours.

To serve, remove springform or rings and peel off parchment paper. Press toasted nuts or sliced almonds onto sides of charlotte.

131

Tarte Tatin

WE'VE ADDED A FEW ingredients to this classic apple tart. By caramelizing butter and brown sugar with cinnamon and brandy, the result is a tart with a great amount of flavor. This tart can also be prepared ahead of time, chilled in the baking pan, and reheated before being turned out onto a platter.

Makes 1 10-inch (25-cm) tart

½	recipe Puff Pastry (page 125)	½
6	Mutsu or Granny Smith apples	6
¼ cup	unsalted butter	60 mL
½ cup	brown sugar	120 mL
½ tsp.	cinnamon	2.5 mL
1 Tbsp.	brandy or Calvados	15 mL

Preheat oven to 375°F (190°C). Roll out pastry to ¼ inch (.6 cm) thick on a lightly floured surface and cut a disc the size of a 10-inch (25-cm) tart shell. Chill until ready to use. Peel, core and cut apples into quarters.

Melt butter in a medium sauté pan over medium-high heat. As soon as butter is melted, add brown sugar and cinnamon, stirring until blended and bubbling. Add brandy (watch out for flames) and stir. Spoon into a pie pan (not removable bottom). Arrange apples on top of sugar. Make holes in pastry with a fork and place on top of apples.

Place pie pan on a baking sheet, to avoid any drips onto oven floor. Bake for 25 to 30 minutes, until crust is rich golden brown and apples are tender. Turn out onto a platter, so that apples are on top. Watch for hot syrup that might drip.

Mutsu apples are my favorite. They are great for cooking, delicious raw, and grow in abundance in the Niagara region. Peaches are also delicious, and in August and September I use this recipe for Peach Tarte Tatin.

132

Lemon Mousse Crepes

INSTEAD OF SERVING lemon mousse in a cup at the restaurant, we pipe it into crepes, which look like soufflé pancakes, but taste cool and refreshing. This dessert is for people who are not big dessert eaters. Not overly sweet or heavy, the mousse cleanses the palate after a great meal.

Serves 6

	zest of 1 lemon	
1/4 cup	lemon juice	60 mL
1 1/2 tsp.	gelatin powder	7.5 mL
3	eggs	3
3 Tbsp.	sugar	45 mL
1/2 cup	whipping cream	120 mL
1 Tbsp.	sour cream	15 mL
12	6-inch (15-cm) crepes (see page 126)	12

Place lemon zest, juice and gelatin in a small pan, allowing gelatin to soften a minute. Dissolve gelatin over low heat and set aside. In a mixer fitted with whisk attachment, whip eggs with sugar until they leave a "ribbon" on themselves when whisk is lifted. Whip cream to soft peaks and fold in sour cream. Fold cream into egg mixture. Turn mixer on low speed and pour in lemon gelatin in a thin stream, but not too slowly.

Pour mousse into a container and chill for 2 hours. Check after 1 hour that lemon juice has not settled to the bottom. If it has, simply fold over mousse to incorporate it.

To serve, spoon mousse into a piping bag fitted with a large star tip. Lay out crepes on a work surface and pipe mousse in a spiral over one side of crepes (semi-circle). Fold other half of crepe to cover mousse and chill until ready to use.

If you don't have a piping bag with tips, there's no need to skip this recipe. Simply spoon the mousse onto half of the crepe and fold over for the same effect.

133

Mae Olson's Vinetarta

A PART OF MANY Icelandic-Canadian special occasions, this cake should be portioned into small, two-bite pieces. It is fantastic served with a pot of coffee.

The cake is built with 5 layers, each of which is baked separately. Michael's mother, Mae Olson, had 5 cake tins that were reserved for making vinetarta, but you can use one or two cake pans, and bake the layers in a few batches.

Makes 1 12-inch (30-cm) cake

Filling

1 lb.	pitted prunes	455 g
3/4 cup	sugar	180 mL
1/2 cup	reserved soaking liquid from prunes	120 mL
1 Tbsp.	cinnamon	15 mL
1 Tbsp.	vanilla extract	15 mL

Cake

1 cup	unsalted butter	240 mL
1 1/2 cups	sugar	360 mL
2	eggs	2
1 tsp.	baking powder	5 mL
3 Tbsp.	half-and-half cream	45 mL
3/4 tsp.	almond extract	4 mL
1 tsp.	ground cardamom	5 mL
4 cups	all purpose flour	950 mL

To prepare cake, preheat oven to 350°F (175°C). Lightly butter cake pans. In a bowl or mixer fitted with paddle attachment, cream butter. Add sugar gradually and beat until smooth. Beat in eggs one at a time. Add sifted baking powder. Add cream and flavorings and work in flour. Dough will resemble a shortbread.

Divide dough into 5 equal parts. Pat each piece of dough into a cake pan. Bake until delicately browned, 12 to 15 minutes. Allow to cool a few minutes before removing from pan.

To prepare filling, cover prunes with water in a saucepot and simmer for 10 minutes. Drain liquid, reserving ½ cup (120 mL). Purée prunes in a food processor. Spoon purée back into pot and add reserved liquid and remaining ingredients. Cook over low heat, stirring regularly, until filling becomes thick. Allow to cool before filling cake.

To assemble, alternate cake layers with equal amounts of prune filling, finishing with a top cake layer. For special occasions, cake is iced with softened butter beaten with icing sugar and vanilla. Refrigerate cake before serving. As the cake chills, the layers will soften.

135

Taste and smell are such intense memory keys. Michael has said that he immediately associates vinelarla with Christmas as a child. After one taste he wants to put on flannel cowboy pajamas, tear open parcels and shout, "Mine, mine, mine! Gimme, gimme, gimme!"

Panna Cotta

THIS DESSERT IS A GREAT FOIL for summer fruits: in June it is paired with succulent strawberries, in July with three colors of raspberries, and in August with peaches and blackberries.
Makes 6 individual desserts

2 tsp.	gelatin powder	10 mL
1 cup	sour cream	240 mL
1 cup	whipping cream	240 mL
1 cup	half-and-half cream	240 mL
1/3 cup	sugar	80 mL
1	vanilla bean	1

Lightly oil 6 4-oz. (150-mL) ramekins. Soften gelatin in 2 Tbsp. (30 mL) cold water. Place 3 creams and sugar into a medium saucepan. Slice vanilla bean lengthwise and scrape out seeds into cream. Add whole bean to cream for additional flavor.

Bring cream to a simmer, whisking occasionally, and remove vanilla bean pod. Stir in gelatin. Pour into ramekins and chill for 4 hours. To serve, loosen edges of mold with a paring knife, and turn onto a serving plate.

Plum Galette

RUSTIC IN APPEARANCE, galettes pack a punch of flavor, especially the spicy characteristic of plums.
Makes 1 12-inch (30-cm) free-form tart

1	recipe Galette Dough (page 126)	1
2 1/2 cups	purple plums, pitted	600 mL
1/4 cup	sugar	60 mL
1/4 cup	light brown sugar	60 mL
1/4 tsp.	cinnamon	1.2 mL
1 Tbsp.	butter	15 mL
1	egg, mixed with water for brushing	1

Preheat oven to 375°F (190°C). On a lightly floured surface, roll out galette dough to a 1/4-inch-thick (.6-cm) circle.

In a bowl, mix together plums, sugars and cinnamon. Center this mixture on the dough, leaving 4 inches (10 cm) around the outside edge. Dot plums with butter and fold crust over them, overlapping folds. It will take 5 or 6 folds to complete tart.

Place tart on a parchment-lined baking sheet. Brush crust with egg wash and sprinkle with granulated sugar. Bake for 25 to 35 minutes, until crust is golden brown and plums are bubbling.

Raspberry Rhubarb Custard Tart

THIS CUSTARD FILLING is not a traditional pastry cream. The raw custard is poured over the fruit, then sets as it mixes with the juices. Rhubarb with raspberry produces a tart of vibrant pink color.

Makes 1 10-inch (25-cm) tart

Crust

¹⁄₄ cup	ground almonds	60 mL
1¹⁄₂ cups	all purpose flour	360 mL
¹⁄₂ cup	sugar	120 mL
1 Tbsp.	brown sugar	15 mL
¹⁄₄ tsp.	salt	1.2 mL
²⁄₃ cup	unsalted butter	160 mL
¹⁄₂ tsp.	vanilla	2.5 mL

Fruit Filling

1¹⁄₂ cups	rhubarb, diced	360 mL
1 cup	raspberries	240 mL

Custard

¹⁄₄ cup	whipping cream	60 mL
1	egg	1
¹⁄₄ cup	sugar	60 mL
2 Tbsp.	all purpose flour	30 mL
1 Tbsp.	ground almonds	15 mL
1 Tbsp.	brandy	15 mL
dash	vanilla extract	dash

Preheat oven to 350°F (175°C). In a bowl or an electric mixer fitted with paddle attachment, combine almonds, flour, sugars and salt. Cut in butter and vanilla until texture is crumbly. Reserve ²⁄₃ cup (160 mL) of crumble and press remaining crumble into an ungreased 10-inch (25-cm) springform pan. Bake for 20 minutes and allow to cool.

Mix rhubarb and raspberries and place them on crust. Whisk together custard ingredients and pour over berries. Sprinkle reserved crumble on top of fruit and bake for 20 to 30 minutes, until custard has set. Tart can be served at room temperature or chilled.

Lemon Tart

WE HAVE INCLUDED 2 methods for lemon tart: the classic French Tarte au Citron, and a lemon curd tart. Both are refreshing, palate-cleansing desserts and both have been served at the restaurant with popular response. The French-style filling is baked in the tart shell, whereas the lemon curd filling is prepared on the stove and then piped into the shell. The choice is yours.

Sugar pastry does not need to be rolled ice cold. In fact, it is difficult to do so as it often cracks. Let the sugar dough come up to just below room temperature before rolling, or knead it for a few minutes to loosen it.
Makes 1 10-inch (25-cm) tart

1	recipe Sugar Pastry (page 124)	1

French-style Filling

$\frac{1}{3}$ cup	lemon juice	80 mL
$\frac{1}{2}$ cup	sugar	120 mL
4	eggs	4
1 cup	whipping cream	240 mL
1 Tbsp.	lemon zest	15 mL

Lemon Curd Filling

$\frac{1}{2}$ cup	sugar	120 mL
2	eggs	2
1	egg yolk	1
$\frac{1}{2}$ cup	lemon juice	120 mL
$\frac{1}{4}$ cup	unsalted butter	60 mL
1 Tbsp.	lemon zest	15 mL

138

Preheat oven to 375°F (190°C). On a lightly floured surface, roll out sugar pastry to $\frac{1}{4}$ inch (.6 cm) thick. Line a 10-inch (25-cm) removable-bottom tart shell with dough and chill for 30 minutes. Prick crust with a fork and bake for 15 to 20 minutes, until edges are lightly browned and center is dry. Allow to cool.

To prepare French-style filling, reduce oven temperature to 325°F (165°C). Whisk together lemon juice, sugar, eggs, whipping cream and lemon zest and pour them into tart shell. Bake for 25 to 30 minutes, until outside of tart filling is set but center is still slightly soft. The tart will finish setting after it is out of the oven. Allow tart to cool and chill for at least 2 hours before serving.

To prepare lemon curd filling, place a pot with 2 inches (5 cm) of water to simmer over the stove. In a metal bowl, whisk together sugar, eggs, egg yolk and lemon juice. Cut butter into small pieces and whisk them in. Place bowl over simmering water and whisk until sauce thickens, 10 to 12 minutes. Strain curd and stir in zest. Place a piece of plastic wrap directly touching tart surface and chill for at least 2 hours. Pipe or spoon curd into tart shell and chill before serving.

The traditional Tarte au Citron is often served caramelized. To do this, sprinkle the top of the chilled tart with superfine sugar and broil for 30 to 45 seconds, or brown with a blowtorch (this may be hard to get hold of if you are serving time for arson in a federal penitentiary).

The lemon curd tart is the base for a lemon meringue pie. If you wish, top the tart with 3 egg whites whipped with $\frac{3}{4}$ cup (180 mL) sugar and bake for 15 minutes, or top with chantilly cream.

139

Blueberry Minted Custard Tart

THE COMBINATION OF MINT and fresh blueberries makes a very refreshing tart. If you are making an individual tart, the blueberries can be stacked on top of each other and held together with melted apricot jelly to create a tower of berries!

Makes 1 10-inch (25-cm) tart

¹⁄₂	recipe Sugar Pastry (full recipe if making individual tarts) (page 124)	¹⁄₂
1	recipe Pastry Cream (page 129)	1
1 Tbsp.	finely chopped fresh mint	15 mL
2 cups	fresh blueberries	480 mL
	icing sugar for dusting	

Preheat oven to 375°F (190°C). Roll out sugar pastry to ¹⁄₄ inch (.6 cm) thick and line a removable-bottom tart shell with it. Chill pastry for ¹⁄₂ hour. Blindbake crust for 15 minutes. Remove weights and bake 5 minutes more, until crust is light golden brown. Allow to cool.

When making pastry cream recipe, add mint to the milk as it is heating. Otherwise, mint can be folded in once pastry cream has cooled. Spoon cream into tart shell and arrange blueberries on top. Dust lightly with icing sugar through a shaker and serve.

These tarts look absolutely beautiful arranged on a big plate; we display them at the front desk of Inn on the Twenty to remind people of dessert. Customers end up looking like children peering into the window of a candy shop.

140

Apricot Cream Cheese Tart

APRICOTS ARE GREAT for baking since they hold their shape and don't leak juices. This simple tart has a cheesecake texture that lends itself well to the delicate apricot.

Makes 1 10-inch (25-cm) tart or 6 individual tarts

½	recipe Sugar Pastry (full recipe if making individual tarts) (page 124)	½
8 oz.	cream cheese, softened	225 g
¾ cup	sugar	120 mL
2 Tbsp.	whipping cream	30 mL
1	egg	1
1 Tbsp.	all purpose flour	15 mL
1 tsp.	vanilla extract	5 mL
6–8	fresh apricots, pitted and halved	6–8

Preheat oven to 375°F (190°C). Roll out sugar pastry to ¼ inch (.6 cm) thick and line a removable-bottom tart shell or shells with it. Chill pastry for half an hour. Blindbake crust for 15 minutes. Remove weights and bake 5 minutes more, until crust is light golden brown. Allow to cool.

Reduce oven temperature to 350°F (175°C). Beat cream cheese until smooth. Add sugar and cream. Blend in egg, flour and vanilla. Pour mixture into tart shell and arrange apricots on top. Bake for 20 to 25 minutes, until cream cheese mixture soufflés and browns lightly.

Cave Spring Indian Summer Riesling is a late harvest wine that always marries well with apricot desserts.

141

Niagara Fruit Cobbler

A STAPLE DESSERT at Inn on the Twenty and easy to make at home, since almost any fruit or combination can be used. We most often use an apple or peach base with berries as an accent. The apples hold their shape, keep the cobbler suspended and absorb the abundance of berry juices.

Serves 8

2 cups	Mutsu apples, peeled and diced	475 mL
1½ cups	mixed berries, such as raspberries, blueberrries, blackberries or cherries	360 mL
½ cup	sugar	120 mL
½ tsp.	cinnamon	2.5 mL
2 cups	all purpose flour	475 mL
3 Tbsp.	cornmeal	45 mL
⅔ cup	sugar	160 mL
2 tsp.	baking powder	10 mL
¼ tsp.	salt	1.2 mL
⅔ cup	unsalted butter, cut into pieces and chilled	160 mL
	zest of 1 lemon	
⅔ cup	milk	160 mL
1 tsp.	vanilla extract	5 mL

Preheat oven to 325°F (165°C). Toss fruit with ½ cup (120 mL) sugar and cinnamon. Pour fruit into an 8-cup (2-L) casserole dish.

In a mixing bowl or in an electric mixer fitted with paddle attachment, combine flour, cornmeal, ⅔ cup (160 mL) sugar, baking powder and salt. Cut in butter until the texture resembles coarse meal. Add lemon zest, milk and vanilla and combine until dough is evenly mixed. Spoon dough over fruit, leaving a few spaces for expansion. Bake for 45 minutes to 1 hour. Serve warm with Chantilly Cream (page 129) or ice cream.

> *We like to serve this cobbler baked in coffee cups, with a spoonful of chantilly cream on top. For a kick, add ½ cup grated cheddar cheese to the topping of your apple cobbler.*

142

Lemon Mascarpone and Strawberry Wedding Cake

WHAT A GLORIOUS OCCASION! What a glorious cake! Pristine and simply decorated on the exterior, it is a delight to behold the interior: two layers of delicate, lemon-scented cake filled with rich lemon mascarpone mousse. Nestled in the mousse are whole strawberries, so that once the cake is sliced, the heart-shaped berries are visible. The cake is finished with a true buttercream and beautifully decorated with flowers, ribbon and piping.

To prepare this cake, give yourself 3 days. The first day to bake the cake and set the mousse, the second day to ice the cake, and the third day for the finishing touches. If you are preparing this cake for a friend, a family member, or yourself, you do want to give yourself enough time to enjoy the process and be satisfied with the result. The techniques involved are not difficult, but patience is required in the assembly and finishing steps.

Some tools used in this recipe, while not exotic, may not be found in every kitchen but can be purchased at a specialty cake store.

Good luck and enjoy your creation!

Serves 50 as a dessert course, or 80 as a taste

Tools Required

- 2 10-inch (25-cm) round cake pans, preferably springform
- 2 14-inch (36-cm) round cake pans, preferably springform
- 2 cardboard cake rounds, 1 10-inch (25-cm), 1 14-inch (36-cm)
- 1 16-inch (40-cm) cake platter
- Offset spatula
- Piping bags
- $\frac{1}{8}$ inch (.3 cm) plain piping tip
- $\frac{1}{2}$ inch (1.2 cm) plain piping tip
- Bamboo skewers
- 8 feet (2.4 m) of $1\frac{1}{2}$-inch-wide (4-cm) ribbon
- Parchment paper
- Floral tape

143

Lemon Cake

2 cups	unsalted butter, at room temperature	475 mL
4 cups	sugar	950 mL
1½ Tbsp.	vanilla extract	22.5 mL
	zest of 4 lemons	
6¾ cups	cake flour	1.7 L
2½ Tbsp.	baking powder	37.5 mL
1 tsp.	baking soda	5 mL
1 tsp.	salt	5 mL
12	egg whites	12
1½ cups	milk	360 mL
1½ cups	buttermilk	360 mL

This batter can be mixed by hand in a very large bowl, or split into 2 batches and prepared in an electric mixer fitted with the paddle attachment. If you are making the batter in batches, it can be baked all at once. The first batch of batter will not be affected if it sits at room temperature for a little while.

Preheat oven to 350°F (175°C). Lightly grease all 4 cake pans and line bottoms and sides with parchment paper.

In a large bowl or mixer, beat butter until fluffy. Gradually add sugar and mix until pale in color. Beat in vanilla and lemon zest.

In a separate bowl, sift together flour, baking powder, baking soda and salt. In a separate bowl, whisk together egg whites with milk and buttermilk. Do not worry if mixture looks slightly curdled, it will smooth out in the end.

Add ⅓ of the dry ingredients to the butter mixture and beat until incorporated. Add ⅓ of the milk mixture and mix until evenly blended. Repeat until all ingredients are incorporated and batter is smooth. If using a mixer, be sure to scrape down the sides of the bowl frequently.

Spoon batter evenly into the cake pans and bake for 35 to 45 minutes, until a skewer inserted into the center of the cake comes out clean. Be sure to check the smaller cakes first, as they may not take as long to bake.

Remove cakes from oven and allow to cool. If cake is not being filled until the next day, wrap the cakes with plastic wrap and leave at room temperature. Refrigerating cakes will dry them out.

This cake recipe has great flavor, stays moist and is not complicated to make. Cut this recipe in half to make 2 12-inch (30-cm) layers. It's as easy as baking a cake!

Lemon Mascarpone Mousse Filling

4	2-cup (500-mL) tubs mascarpone cheese	4
4 cups	whipping cream	950 mL
2 cups	sugar	475 mL
1½ cups	lemon juice	360 mL
	zest of 4 lemons	

Place mascarpone in a large bowl and beat with a spatula to smooth. In an electric mixer fitted with whisk attachment, or with a hand-held mixer, whip cream to soft peaks. Fold together cream with mascarpone and add sugar, lemon juice and zest. Mix vigorously until just smooth, about 4 minutes by hand or 1 minute by mixer. Do not overmix or the mousse may curdle. Chill until ready to use.

> ✿ *Do be sure to buy the best quality of mascarpone cheese you can find; it should be smooth in texture (not granular), and usually over 40% in milk fat. While you may be conscious of cutting back on fat, this is one occasion where the more fat, the better!*

To Fill Cake

| | icing sugar, for dusting | |
| 3 quarts | fresh strawberries, washed and hulled | 3 L |

Remove cake layers from pans and peel away parchment. Lightly dust cakes on all sides with icing sugar so they do not stick to the table.

Wash cake pans and line the bottom of one of each size with a cardboard cake round. Line the sides of the pans with a 5-inch-tall (12.5-cm) tall piece of parchment paper (do not grease the sides of the pans). Place one layer of each cake into the pans, bottom-side down. Using the offset spatula, spread a thin layer of mascarpone mousse over the cakes. Arrange strawberries over mousse, leaving ¼ inch (.6 cm) between each berry. It is easiest to begin by lining the outside perimeter of the cake with strawberries and working inward.

Fill a piping bag fitted with the ½-inch (1.2-cm) tip with mousse and pipe generously into the spaces between the berries and over top. Smooth mousse with a spatula to create a level surface. Place remaining cake layers on top of mousse, bottom-side up, and press gently to ensure cakes are level. Wrap loosely with plastic wrap and chill overnight.

You will need to make two batches of buttercream, so have on hand double quantities of the ingredients listed below. Leave the first batch at room temperature while making the second batch.

Buttercream

8	egg whites, at room temperature	8
½ tsp.	cream of tartar	2.5 mL
dash	salt	dash
1½ cups + 2 Tbsp.	sugar	390 mL
3 cups	unsalted butter, at room temperature	720 mL
½ Tbsp.	vanilla extract	7.5 mL

In a clean bowl of an electric mixer fitted with whisk attachment, whip together egg whites, cream of tartar and salt until frothy. Gradually add ¾ cup (180 mL) of sugar to whites and whip until they reach soft peaks.

In a saucepot, place remaining sugar and 1 cup (240 mL) of water over high heat and bring to a boil. Using a sugar or digital thermometer, cook sugar syrup until it reaches 240°F (117°C). With mixer on medium-high speed, carefully and slowly pour sugar syrup into egg whites, letting the syrup run down the side of the bowl into the whites. Whip whites on high speed to cool them to room temperature. This takes 10 to 15 minutes.

Reduce mixer speed to medium and, a cup at a time, add butter, stopping frequently to scrape the sides of the mixing bowl. Buttercream may appear slightly curdled at first, but the longer you whip it, the smoother it will get. Beat in vanilla.

This definitely is one of those recipes that warrants licking the bowl and beater after it has been made. The joy in making buttercream in two batches? Two bowls to lick!

146

To Ice Cake

Buttercream must be at room temperature to use. Set aside 1 cup (240 mL) for piping details.

Remove cakes from first cake pan and gently peel away parchment. Using the offset spatula, smooth a thin layer of buttercream over the sides and then the top of the cake. Don't worry if you can see through the icing; this layer is called a "crumb coat" and serves to even any imperfections and avoid crumbs getting onto the outside of the cake. Chill in the refrigerator and repeat process with the other cakes.

Once the first tier is set, spread on another layer of buttercream, this time taking more care that it is evenly distributed and generally smooth, first on the sides, and then on the top. Using the flat side of the spatula, drag it along the outside perimeter of the cake, to remove excess icing and create a sharp corner at the top.

Fill a pitcher with boiling water and submerge spatula. Dry the hot spatula with paper towel and, working a section at a time around the cake, smooth out the buttercream. The heat of the spatula melts any bubbles or lines away. Once the spatula cools, insert in hot water, dry and repeat. Follow this technique along the top of the cake. Give yourself plenty of time for this step and take breaks. Do not chill cake while resting, though, as retouching the icing may be more difficult once it is set.

Once you are content with the smooth finish of your cake, repeat with the second tier. Do remember that the larger cake will have the smaller tier placed on top of it, and while the top of the cake does not have to be as polished-looking as the top layer, it must be level. Be sure to look at your cake from all angles. Chill layers for 1 hour before stacking.

To stack tiers, remove larger cake from the refrigerator. Place 1 of the 4 skewers about 6 inches (15 cm) from the edge of the cake and

147

stick it through the cake until it touches the bottom. Mark with a pencil where the skewer breaks the surface of the cake. Slice skewer at that line and cut the other 3 skewers to that length. Stick all of the skewers into bottom layer in a square pattern near the center of the cake. While this mousse cake is very stable, the skewers will prevent any settling that might crack the set buttercream.

Remove the smaller cake from the refrigerator and center it on the larger layer. If you must, you can measure 2 inches (5 cm) into the large tier, and mark the icing gently to show where the smaller tier should be placed. Fill in any cracks with icing and smooth with a hot spatula. Chill cake for 1 hour.

To Decorate Cake

Fill a piping bag fitted with the $\frac{1}{8}$-inch (.3-cm) tip with buttercream. Place cake on desired platter. Cut a length of parchment the width of the ribbon being used and wrap around the bottom of each tier. This will prevent the buttercream from leaving any oil marks on the ribbon. Wrap ribbon around cake and secure at the back with a touch of buttercream.

Beginning at the bottom tier, pipe tiny dots along the lower edge of the ribbon, slowly working around the cake. Buttercream dots are not permanent, so if you make a mistake, simply scrape off the dots and begin again.

Repeat this step over the top edge of the ribbon, on both tiers and on the outside edge of the top of cake. Dots can be omitted or added anywhere you please. Chill cake 1 hour.

Flowers should be added to the cake no more than 4 to 6 hours before it is displayed. To arrange flowers, trim stems to 1 to $1\frac{1}{2}$ inches (2.5 to 4 cm) from the bud. Using floral tape, wrap stems tightly with tape to secure. Arrange flowers as desired, be it symmetrically on top or draping over the edges. Use greenery to fill in any spaces. This is purely subjective decorating and is how you personalize your cake. Do bear in mind that balance in color and texture creates eye appeal.

❧ Send out the cake to the bride and groom with congratulations, then sit back and congratulate yourself!

Lavender Blueberry Sauce

THE SUMMERY FLAVOR of lavender is a wonderful accent to blueberries. When lavender blooms, its flavor is at its strongest, so only 2 sprigs may be needed (add the flowers and all). This sauce is improved only by serving it with a cool lemon dessert, such as Lemon Mousse Crepes or Lemon Tart.
Yields 2 cups (475 mL)

2 cups	blueberries, fresh or frozen	475 mL
$3/4$ cup	sugar	180 mL
2–3	sprigs lavender	2–3
$1\frac{1}{2}$ tsp.	lemon juice	7.5 mL

In a saucepot, bring to a simmer $1\frac{1}{2}$ cups (360 mL) blueberries, sugar, lavender and lemon juice. Simmer for 10 minutes and remove from heat. Remove lavender stems and purée sauce with a hand blender or in a food processor.

Add remaining blueberries and bring back to a simmer. Sauce can be served warm or chilled.

Raspberry Sauce

MADE WITH FRESH or frozen berries, the refreshing taste of red raspberries highlights many sweets.

While the idea of making a sauce from golden raspberries may seem appealing, the sparkling color of the fresh berries fades when cooked and blended, and the low acidity in the fruit results in a less than appealing taste. Red raspberries work best, although black raspberries can also be used satisfactorily.
Yields 2 cups (475 mL)

3 cups	red raspberries, fresh or frozen	720 mL
$2/3$ cup	sugar	160 mL
	zest of 1 lemon	

Simmer all ingredients for 10 to 15 minutes, just enough to melt and incorporate the sugar. Purée and strain. Chill sauce before serving.

> *A coulis is made from fresh fruit, whereas a fruit sauce is cooked. The advantages of a sauce over a coulis are that the texture is smoother, the color glossier and a sauce has a longer shelf life in the refrigerator (up to 5 days), where a coulis may only last 2 to 3 days.*

Crème Anglaise

A BASIC CUSTARD SAUCE, this dessert accompaniment is very adaptable. Cool or warm, crème anglaise is especially delicious with fruit tarts.

Yields 1$\frac{1}{3}$ cups (320 mL)

1 cup	half-and-half cream	240 mL
$\frac{1}{2}$	vanilla bean	$\frac{1}{2}$
	or	
1 tsp.	pure vanilla extract	5 mL
2	egg yolks	2
3 Tbsp.	sugar	45 mL

In a small saucepot, heat cream and the scraped seeds of the vanilla bean (and the pod for additional flavor) or vanilla extract. Heat cream to a scald (until it gets a skin on top) over medium heat.

In a bowl, whisk together egg yolks and sugar. A spoonful at a time, whisk a little hot cream into the egg mixture, whisking constantly, until all the cream is added.

Return pot to low heat and stir with a wooden spoon until the sauce coats the back of the spoon evenly, 4 to 6 minutes. Strain and chill.

 Custard sauces do not need to be complicated, but you do want to avoid overcooking your eggs. You can usually tell that crème anglaise is close to being cooked when the small bubbles that were created when whisking the sauce disappear as the sauce thickens.

The simple flavor of a basic crème anglaise can be enhanced to adapt to any dessert you may be serving. We recommend any of the following:
- *1 Earl Grey or Orange Pekoe tea bag*
- *1 tsp. (5 mL) instant coffee*
- *1 bay leaf (great with chocolate)*
- *2 mint or lemon balm sprigs*
- *zest of 1 orange*
- *2 tsp. (10 mL) Ovaltine (reduce sugar in recipe by half for this option)*

Roasted Apricot Sauce
with Vanilla

ROASTING THIS DELICATE FRUIT for sauce concentrates the flavor and the vanilla adds a robust character that stands up to many desserts, such as warm apple pie, cheesecake or chocolate cake.

Yields 2 cups (475 mL)

1 lb.	fresh apricots, halved and pitted	455 g
1/3 cup	sugar	80 mL
1/3 cup	brown sugar	80 mL
	juice of 1 lemon	
1	vanilla bean	1

Preheat oven to 350°F (175°C). Toss apricots in a bowl with sugars, lemon juice and scraped seeds from vanilla bean.

Pour onto a lightly greased baking sheet and bake for 20 minutes, until apricots are soft and juice runs when they are pressed. If sugars are not fully dissolved, simmer fruit and sugars in a saucepot until melted.

Purée the apricots with a hand blender or in a food processor and strain.

This sauce is best chilled before serving.

Few flavors conjure up such comfortable memories as vanilla. When purchasing vanilla beans, look for a plump bean that is soft to the touch. To expose the seeds, slice the bean lengthwise and scrape out the seeds using the dull side of a paring knife. Even after use, the vanilla bean itself still has a great deal of flavor. Put the used bean in a tightly closed jar filled with sugar and let it sit for at least a week. Then, if you are out of vanilla, you can replace plain sugar with this flavored one for a delicious result.

Try a spoonful in your next cup of coffee!

151

Caramel

WARM OR COOL, caramel goes with apples.
Yields 1½ cups (360 mL)

1 cup	sugar	240 mL
¼ cup	water	60 mL
⅔ cup	whipping cream	160 mL
½ tsp.	vanilla extract	2.5 mL

In a saucepan over high heat, bring sugar and water to a boil. With a brush dipped in ice water, brush sides of pot frequently to clean any sugar splashes that may occur. Do not stir. Boil until sugar turns a medium golden brown. Sugar will continue to cook after it has been removed from heat, and will darken further.

Whisk in cream, a little at a time (it will bubble up). Allow to cool and stir in vanilla. Caramel sauce may be prepared ahead and easily reheated over the stove or in the microwave.

Apple Raisin Hard Sauce

ROASTED APPLES ADD SPARK to an already festive sauce. Try it with apple desserts or simply spooned over ice cream.
Yields 3 cups (720 mL)

2	Mutsu apples, peeled and diced	2
½ cup	unsalted butter	120 mL
1 cup	brown sugar	240 mL
½ tsp.	cinnamon	2.5 mL
¼ cup	brandy	60 mL
¼ cup	whipping cream	60 mL
½ cup	raisins	120 mL

Preheat oven to 375°F (190°C). Place diced apples on an ungreased baking sheet and roast until light golden brown, 20 to 30 minutes. Allow to cool.

In a heavy-bottomed saucepan, melt butter over medium heat. Add brown sugar and cinnamon and increase temperature to medium-high. Stir until butter and sugar blend together. Carefully add brandy (be cautious of flames) and simmer for 2 minutes. Add cream to sauce and return to a simmer. Remove from heat and stir in the raisins and apples.

Serve sauce warm. Hard sauce will keep for over a week refrigerated and can be reheated on the stove or in the microwave.

If you do not wish your sauce to be "hard," substitute apple cider for the brandy.

152

Indian Summer Riesling Sabayon

THIS CLASSIC SAUCE is delicious served warm over fruit, or cool with a fruit tart. Because it is traditionally prepared with Marsala wine, it is a great conduit between a fruit dessert and the wine served with it. The texture of sabayon is light and airy, and shows the delicate fruitiness of dessert wine well.

If you are serving the sauce warm, it must be prepared immediately before serving, but if it is to be served chilled, the sabayon can be made ahead of time.

Yields 2¹/₂ cups (600 mL)

4	egg yolks	4
¹/₄ cup	lemon juice	60 mL
¹/₄ cup	late harvest Riesling wine	60 mL
¹/₄ cup	sugar	60 mL
2 Tbsp.	whipping cream (optional)	30 mL

Bring a pot with 2 inches (5 cm) of water to a simmer. In a metal bowl, whisk together yolks, lemon juice, Riesling and sugar. Place bowl over water and whisk briskly until sauce leaves a "ribbon" when whisk is lifted, about 5 minutes.

If serving the sabayon warm, do not add cream but simply spoon sauce over fresh fruit. To prepare for chilling, remove from heat, whisk in cream and chill until ready to serve.

Indian Summer Riesling is a Cave Spring late harvest wine with a moderately high sugar content. Since you've opened the bottle to prepare this recipe, be sure to have a taste yourself!

The base flavor of sabayon can be easily altered by replacing the Riesling with:
- *¹/₄ cup (60 mL) lemon juice for a citrus sauce*
- *¹/₄ cup (60 mL) apple cider to pair with apple desserts*
- *2 Tbsp. (30 mL) balsamic vinegar to highlight fresh strawberries*
- *¹/₄ cup (60 mL) rum and a dash of nutmeg for a holiday eggnog sauce.*

153

BREAD AND BREAKFAST

Since the Vintner's Inn opened in 1996, we open for breakfast at 8 o'clock every morning. Guests are offered a selection of freshly baked goods, homemade granola, fruit and hot items from the kitchen. Visitors walking from their rooms across the street to the dining room are encouraged by the smells of sticky buns and sourdough wafting through the village.

Before most people are awake, Anna and her pastry shop team are busy coaxing different doughs into loaves, boules, baguettes and knots. Enough people asking for our bread led us to sell it on weekends through the wine store.

As any cook turned baker will agree, the first time you make a loaf of bread, it is the most gratifying cooking experience imaginable. Something so basic to western culture and yet so much taken for granted in busy modern life, baking bread is a very satisying accomplishment indeed.

You will notice that many of the bread components in this section are weighed instead of measured. The precision of weighing guarantees a consistent and successful result.

155

Sunflower Bread

THIS IS A VERY POPULAR recipe at the restaurant. The addition of molasses adds a touch of sweetness and softens the texture of the bread, making it great for sandwiches.
Makes 2 loaves

3 cups + 2 Tbsp.	warm water 105°F (40°C)	750 mL
½ oz.	dry active yeast	14 g
1½ oz.	blackstrap molasses	42 g
8¾ oz.	whole wheat flour	250 g
2 lbs. 2 oz.	organic bread flour	1 kg
1 oz.	salt	28 g
2 oz.	raw sunflower seeds	56 g

In the bowl of an electric mixer fitted with the dough hook, sprinkle yeast over water and allow to dissolve, about 5 minutes. Add remaining ingredients and mix on low speed for 3 minutes. Increase speed to medium and knead for 12 minutes. Dough should just clean the sides of the mixing bowl. Place dough in a lightly oiled bowl, cover and allow to rise in a warm place, about 85°F (29°C), for 1 hour.

Turn dough out onto a lightly floured surface and knock down. Divide dough in half, and roll into 2 rounds. Cover and let rest 25 minutes. Shape dough into loaves by rolling (without tearing the surface of the dough) or reshape into rounds and place on a parchment-lined baking sheet. Gently brush with water and allow to rest 20 to 30 minutes, until dough no longer springs back when poked with your finger.

Preheat oven to 400°F (200°C). Brush loaves again with water and score just through the surface. Place in oven and reduce temperature to 350°F (175°C). Bake for 40 minutes, until bread makes a hollow sound when knocked on the bottom. Allow to cool for at least half an hour before cutting.

We use organic flour for baking breads, since it is the most untreated. Many bread flours have activators in them, to assist the yeast in its leavening. These activators, however, remove your power to control how the bread rises, and will sometimes result in an overly "fluffy" loaf. Organic bread flours are becoming more available, but can most commonly be found at natural food stores.

Millet Flaxseed Bread

THIS BREAD RECIPE creates a loaf with a lot of texture, without being overly heavy or dense. While regular honey is called for in this recipe, using buckwheat honey enhances the flavor of the different grains.

Makes 2 loaves

3 cups + 2 Tbsp.	warm water 105°F (40°C)	750 mL
½ oz.	dry active yeast	14 g
8¾ oz.	whole wheat flour	250 g
2 lbs. 2 oz.	organic bread flour	1 kg
1½ oz.	honey	40 g
1 oz.	salt	28 g
2 oz.	whole millet	57 g
1 oz.	flaxseed	28 g

In the bowl of an electric mixer fitted with the dough hook, sprinkle yeast over water and allow to dissolve, about 5 minutes.

Add remaining ingredients and mix on low speed for 3 minutes. Increase speed to medium and knead for 12 minutes. Dough should just clean the sides of the mixing bowl. Allow dough to rise in a lightly oiled bowl, covered, in a warm place, about 85°F (29°C), for 1 hour.

Turn dough out onto a lightly floured surface and knock down. Divide dough in half, and roll into 2 rounds. Cover and let rest 25 minutes. Shape dough into loaves by rolling (without tearing the surface of the dough) or reshape into rounds and place on a parchment-lined baking sheet. Gently brush with water and allow to rest 20 to 30 minutes, until dough no longer springs back when poked with your finger.

Preheat oven to 400°F (200°C). Brush loaves again with water and score just through the surface. Place in oven and reduce temperature to 350°F (175°C). Bake for 40 minutes, until bread makes a hollow sound when knocked on the bottom. Allow to cool for at least half an hour before cutting.

Maybe you have consumed grain breads along this line that have the appeal of the floor scrapings out of a '73 pickup truck, but this loaf is excellent on its own or, even better, as a landing pad for rare roast beef and mustard.

Sourdough Bread

THE PLEASURE IN MAKING bread at home is derived not only from the final result, but from the aroma as it rises and bakes in the oven. Sourdough bread is made using a starter—a mix of flour and water that creates its own leavening ability. As the yeast feeds and ferments, it develops that unique "sour" taste. Give this dough plenty of time to rise— you can't rush good bread.

The sourdough starter must be made at least one day ahead, and fed every third day with more water and flour. Some starters are years old and the longer they age, the more intense a flavor they attain.

Yields 2 loaves

Starter

2 cups	warm water 105°F (40°C)	475 mL
pinch	dry active yeast	pinch
1 lb.	organic bread flour	455 g

Bread

3 cups + 2 Tbsp.	warm water 105°F (40°C)	750 mL
⅓ oz.	dry active yeast	9 g
7 oz.	starter	200 g
2 lbs. 12 oz.	organic bread flour	1.25 kg
¾ oz.	salt	20 g
	cornmeal for dusting	

To make the starter, combine yeast and water and allow to dissolve in the bowl of an electric mixer, about 5 minutes. Add flour and blend until smooth using a paddle attachment.

158

Wrap starter and store in a warm place for a minimum of 12 hours.

To make bread, mix water, yeast and starter in the bowl of an electric mixer fitted with dough hook. Allow yeast to dissolve for 5 minutes. Add flour and salt and mix on low speed for 2 minutes. Increase to medium speed and knead for 12 minutes. Dough should just clean the sides of the bowl. It is good if the dough sticks slightly to the bottom. You may need to add a touch of flour or water to achieve the right consistency.

After kneading, place dough in an oiled bowl and cover. Allow to rise in a warm place 85°F (29°C) for 3 hours. This length of time will allow the yeast to slowly work to produce a chewy texture and develop a great flavor.

Turn dough out onto a lightly floured work surface and cut in half. Knock out the air in the dough (this makes the yeast work more) and shape dough into rounds, creating a smooth outside surface. Place loaves on a parchment-lined baking sheet dusted lightly with cornmeal. Brush lightly with water, cover and allow to rise 1 hour, brushing with water occasionally.

Preheat oven to 400°F (200°C). Score loaves across the top and put them in oven. Turn down oven temperature to 350°F (175°C) and bake bread for 40 to 50 minutes. Bread is done when it makes a hollow sound when tapped on the bottom.

Sourdough can be made with more than just flour and water. Once you get the feel for the texture and rising ability of starters, play with ingredients. At the restaurant, we sometimes use the lees that is strained off the wine – it still has active yeast and adds a tremendous flavor.

Other items you can add to your starter are:
* *yogurt or buttermilk*
* *an onion, cut in half*
* *apple cider*
* *malt extract*

Since starters are stored at room temperature, there is a small risk of them spoiling. You will know without a doubt if your starter has spoiled, for it will smell most distinctly of vinegar.

Walnut Bread

THIS DELICIOUS BREAD is a definite favorite, and incited us to sell bread of all types to our customers. Soaking the walnuts in water adds flavor to the dough and also prevents the walnuts from burning on the surface of the loaf. The butter in this recipe creates a silky texture, but can be omitted (you may have to add a little extra water).

Makes 2 loaves

9 oz.	walnut pieces	250 g
1 $^3/_4$ oz.	blackstrap molasses	50 g
2 cups + 2 Tbsp.	warm water 105°F (40°C)	500 mL
$^1/_3$ oz.	dry active yeast	9 g
3 $^1/_2$ oz.	whole wheat flour	100 g
1 lb. 10 oz.	organic bread flour	750 g
$^3/_4$ oz.	salt	20 g
6 oz.	unsalted butter, cut into pieces	170 g

Combine walnuts, molasses, water and yeast in the bowl of an electric mixer fitted with the dough hook and allow to soak for 10 minutes. Add flours and salt and mix on low speed for 2 minutes. Increase speed and knead for 5 minutes. Add butter, a piece at a time, and continue mixing dough for 10 minutes, making sure that all butter is incorporated. Place in a lightly oiled bowl, cover and let rise in a warm place, about 85°F (29°C), for 1$^1/_2$ hours.

Turn dough onto a lightly floured surface and knock down. Divide dough into 2 pieces and shape into rounds, smoothing the top surface of the dough. Cover and let rest for 30 minutes.

Preheat oven to 400°F (200°C). Shape dough into loaves or rounds again and place on a parchment-lined baking sheet. Brush lightly with water and allow to rise 20 minutes. Brush with water once more and score the top just through the surface of the dough. Place bread in oven and reduce heat to 350°F (175°C). Bake for 40 to 50 minutes. Allow to cool for at least $^1/_2$ hour before cutting.

A good friend and wonderful pastry chef, Dean Cole, gave us this recipe. He told us a helpful trick—this dough can be made the night before. Simply cover it well (leaving room to expand) and keep it in the refrigerator overnight. The next morning, shape it into rounds and let it come up to room temperature before baking.

Brioche

BRIOCHE IS SERVED in the restaurant in different forms on a regular basis – as French toast for breakfast, toasted under mushrooms in brandy cream, as stuffing for Cornish hens or as a lining for warm Brie charlottes. Once made, brioche keeps well in the refrigerator or freezer, because of its butter and egg content.
Makes 2 loaves

½ cup	milk, room temperature	120 mL
1 Tbsp.	yeast	15 mL
2 Tbsp.	rum	30 mL
1½ lbs.	all purpose flour	680 g
2 Tbsp.	sugar	30 mL
1 tsp.	salt	5 mL
6	whole eggs, room temperature	6
12 oz.	unsalted butter, room temperature	340 g
1	egg for egg wash	1

Sprinkle yeast over milk in the bowl of a mixer fitted with the paddle attachment. Allow to dissolve for 5 minutes.

Mix remaining ingredients, except butter and egg wash, on low speed for 5 minutes. Switch to a dough hook and knead on medium speed for 5 minutes.

Add butter a bit at a time until it all has been incorporated. You may have to pull the dough off the hook once or twice to work the butter into it. Knead for 5 minutes more. The dough may look very soft, but it will come together. Place in a bowl, cover, and allow to rise at room temperature for 1 hour, then chill overnight in the refrigerator.

To bake, turn brioche out onto a lightly floured surface and divide dough in half. The dough will be very stiff (since the butter will have chilled). Shape into loaves and place in 2 greased loaf tins (or brioche molds). Allow to rise at room temperature for about 2½ hours, until butter in dough has softened, and brioche has doubled in size.

Preheat oven to 375°F (190°C). Whisk egg with a touch of cold water and brush the surface of the dough. Bake for 50 minutes, until top of the loaf is a deep golden brown. Tip loaves out of loaf pans to cool, to avoid condensation.

Brioche is a great medium for flavor and lends itself well to both savory and sweet additions, such as saffron, roasted garlic, coffee, herbs, vanilla or orange or lemon zest.

161

Julia Hajzak's Potato Bread

IN THE WINTER, we make this bread to accompany hearty soups and stews. A Czech friend of ours said she grew up eating it brushed with butter and sprinkled with coarse salt and caraway seeds.

Makes 1 14- × 18-inch (36- × 46-cm) pan

Dough

2 cups + 2 Tbsp.	warm water 105°F (40°C)	500 mL
1 Tbsp.	dry active yeast	15 mL
2 Tbsp.	cornmeal	30 mL
5 cups	organic bread flour	1.2 L
1 Tbsp.	salt	15 mL
2 Tbsp.	vegetable oil	30 mL

Potato Filling

4	Yukon Gold potatoes, peeled	4
¼ cup	unsalted butter	60 mL
	salt	

To make the dough, dissolve yeast in water in the bowl of an electric mixer fitted with the dough hook. Allow to sit for 5 minutes. Add remaining ingredients and mix on low speed for 3 minutes. Increase speed to medium and knead dough for 12 minutes. Place into a lightly oiled bowl, cover, and allow to rise for 1 hour in a warm place, about 85°F (29°C).

Meanwhile, boil potatoes in salted water and drain well. Mash with butter and salt (or use a ricer) and allow to cool.

Turn dough out onto a lightly floured work surface. Using a rolling pin, roll dough into a rectangle 18 inches (46 cm) by 28 inches (72 cm). Using a spatula, spread potato filling evenly on half of the dough, leaving ½ inch (1.2 cm) around the edges. Turn the uncovered dough over the potatoes. Press gently on the dough to push out any air bubbles. Press the edges of the dough to seal. Let rise for 30 minutes.

Preheat oven to 375°F (190°C). Prick the surface of the dough with a fork and bake on a baking sheet for 30 to 40 minutes, until evenly browned.

My grandmother, Julia, used to make this Slovak bread, called "pagasch," every Christmas Eve. Right after it came out of the oven, she would brush it with melted butter and sprinkle it with sugar.

Leftover mashed potatoes work very well in this recipe. Great combinations to add to the potato filling include:
- *slivers of ham*
- *grated cheddar cheese*
- *chopped rosemary or basil*
- *caramelized onions*
- *roasted garlic*

Icewine Holiday Bread

THIS FESTIVE BRAIDED BREAD looks beautiful on a holiday breakfast table, or sweet plate. Since it does not need refrigeration, it also makes a nice hostess gift.

Makes 2 loaves

⅓ cup	dried cherries	80 mL
⅓ cup	dried apricots	80 mL
⅓ cup	raisins	80 mL
⅓ cup	icewine	80 mL
½ cup	walnuts	120 mL
¼ cup	almonds	60 mL
½ tsp.	cinnamon	2.5 mL
½ tsp.	nutmeg	2.5 mL
½ cup	unsalted butter, room temperature	120 mL
3 Tbsp.	honey	45 mL
1	recipe Brioche dough (page 161)	1
1	egg, for brushing	1

Chop dried cherries and apricots and stir in raisins and icewine. Allow to soak for 20 minutes. Roughly chop walnuts and almonds and add to dried fruits with cinnamon and nutmeg. In another bowl, cream butter with honey. Stir in fruit and nut mixture.

Divide dough in half and roll each piece on a lightly floured surface into a rectangle 12 by 18 inches (30 by 46 cm) and ½ inch (1.2 cm) thick. Spread filling lengthwise on center ⅓ of dough pieces. Make 16 angled slices on either side of the filling. Fold strips over filling, one overlapping the other, to create a braided effect. Place loaves on a parchment-lined baking sheet and allow dough to rise for 1½ hours.

Preheat oven to 375°F (190°C). Whisk together egg with 2 Tbsp. (30 mL) cold water and brush onto surface of the bread. Bake for 30 to 40 minutes until bread is a deep golden brown.

Unlike the fruitcake that you receive and then ship off to the next victim, this loaf is a "keeper." Try a slice with icewine for a late-night treat.

Leek Cornbread

SUITABLE FOR EATING on its own in place of bread or rolls, or used as a stuffing, this recipe is easy to make. If you do not have buttermilk, simply add 1 tsp. (5 mL) of white vinegar to 1 cup (240 mL) of milk.

Makes 1 10-inch (25-cm) round or square pan

1 cup	buttermilk	240 mL
¼ cup	vegetable oil	60 mL
2	eggs	2
1	leek, sliced and washed	1
2 Tbsp.	fresh chives, chopped	30 mL
2 cups	cornmeal	475 mL
1 cup	all purpose flour	240 mL
2 Tbsp.	sugar	30 mL
2 tsp.	baking powder	10 mL
1 tsp.	baking soda	5 mL
¾ tsp.	salt	4 mL

Preheat oven to 375°F (190°C). In a small bowl, whisk together buttermilk, oil, eggs, leek and chives and set aside. In a larger bowl, combine remaining ingredients. Add liquids to flour mixture and blend just until all ingredients are incorporated.

Pour into a greased 10-inch (25 cm) round or square baking pan and bake for 30 minutes, until tester comes out clean.

❧ *A tip for successful quick bread such as this recipe, or for muffins and breakfast loaves, is not to overmix. Blend just until ingredients are mixed (a couple of lumps are even OK) and your breads will turn out tender and evenly risen.*

Pecan Sticky Buns

THE SINFULLY SWEET taste of a sticky bun with a steaming cup of coffee warms you to your toes on a cold morning. Try preparing the dough the night before. Allow the buns to come to room temperature in the morning and bake them. The household will be awake and at your mercy instantly.

Makes 12 buns

Dough

2 tsp.	dry active yeast	10 mL
4 Tbsp.	warm water	60 mL
1/2 cup	milk	120 mL
1	egg	1
2 Tbsp.	sugar	30 mL
2 1/2 cups	all purpose flour	600 mL
1/2 tsp.	salt	2.5 mL
1/2 cup	unsalted butter, room temperature	120 mL
1/2 cup	cream cheese, room temperature	120 mL

Pecan Filling

1 cup	unsalted butter, room temperature	240 mL
1 cup	sugar	240 mL
1 Tbsp.	cinnamon	15 mL
1/2 tsp.	nutmeg	2.5 mL
1 1/2 cups	pecans	360 mL

To prepare dough using a mixer, dissolve yeast in water and allow to sit for 5 minutes. Add milk, egg and sugar and blend. Add flour and salt and mix for 1 minute to combine. Add butter and cream cheese and knead for 5 minutes on medium speed. Place dough in a lightly oiled bowl, cover and let rest 1 hour.

For filling, combine butter, sugar, cinnamon, and nutmeg. Chop 1/2 the pecans and add to mixture. Spread 1/2 the filling in a 9- by 13-inch (23- by 33-cm) baking pan. Arrange remaining pecans over filling.

Preheat oven to 350°F (175°C). Roll out dough into a rectangle 1/2 inch (1.2 cm) thick. Spread remaining filling over the dough and roll up lengthwise. Slice dough into 12 equal portions and arrange them in baking pan, leaving some room between buns. Allow to rise 1/2 an hour. Bake for 20 to 30 minutes.

This is a great motivational tool to get the yard raked or garage cleaned out!

Basic Biscuits

As a breakfast item or as a quick replacement for rolls with lunch or dinner, these easy-to-make biscuits can be adapted to suit any flavor. The following is the basic recipe. The two folding steps in rolling the dough create a tremendously flaky biscuit.

Makes 12 biscuits

3 cups	all purpose flour	720 mL
1/4 cup	sugar	60 mL
1 Tbsp.	baking powder	15 mL
1/2 tsp.	salt	2.5 mL
	zest of 1 lemon	
3/4 cup	unsalted butter, chilled	180 mL
1 cup + 2 Tbsp.	milk	270 mL

Preheat oven to 375°F (190°C). Place all dry ingredients, including lemon zest, in a mixing bowl, or in the bowl of an electric mixer fitted with paddle attachment. Cut butter into dry ingredients until it resembles coarse meal. Add milk and mix until dough just comes together.

Turn dough onto a lightly floured surface. Roll dough twice to 1/2 inch (1.2 cm) thick, each time folding in half. Roll dough to 3/4 inch thick (2 cm) and cut desired shapes. Place onto a greased or parchment-lined baking sheet and brush tops lightly with milk. Bake for 15 to 18 minutes, until tops are nicely browned.

❧ *Many additions can be made to this basic recipe to alter it. Depending on your tastes, try any of the following (or a combination):*

- *1/3 cup (80 mL) raisins or dried cherries*
- *2 Tbsp. (30 mL) brown sugar mixed with 1/2 tsp. (2.5 mL) cinnamon*
- *1/2 cup (120 ml) chocolate chips*
- *glaze tops with maple syrup*
- *2 Tbsp. (30 mL) chopped fresh basil*
- *2 Tbsp. (30 mL) chopped fresh rosemary*
- *1/2 cup (120 mL) grated cheddar cheese*
- *1/2 cup (120 mL) chopped cooked ham or bacon*
- *1/3 cup (80 mL) chopped green onions*
- *1/4 cup (60 mL) chopped pitted olives*
- *1 Tbsp. (15 mL) roasted garlic*

Buttermilk Muffin Mix

HAVING A GOOD MUFFIN recipe presents great flexibility because you can add anything and everything to this base to create a different muffin every day. This recipe can be multiplied and kept in the fridge for up to 5 days. Have a different freshly baked muffin every morning!

Makes 12 muffins

2½ cups	all purpose flour	600 mL
1 tsp.	baking powder	5 mL
1 tsp.	baking soda	5 mL
½ tsp.	salt	2.5 mL
1⅓ cups	brown sugar	320 mL
½ cup	buttermilk	120 mL
½ cup	vegetable oil	120 mL
1	egg	1
1½ tsp.	vanilla extract	7.5 mL

Preheat oven to 375°F (190°C). Combine flour, baking powder, baking soda and salt. In another bowl, blend together brown sugar, buttermilk, oil, egg and vanilla. Add liquids to flour and mix until batter just comes together. Do not overmix.

To bake, stir in desired fruit or flavoring and spoon into greased muffin pans. Bake for 20 minutes, until tops are golden brown. Allow to cool 5 minutes before removing from muffin pan.

Suggested fillings for this muffin recipe include:
- *1 cup (240 mL) fresh raspberries or blueberries*
- *¾ cup (180 mL) cranberries and zest of 1 orange*
- *½ cup (120 mL) pecans and 1/2 tsp. (2.5 mL) cinnamon*
- *¾ cup (180 mL) chocolate chips*
- *½ cup (120 mL) diced apple and ½ cup (120 mL) raisins*
- *1 cup (240 mL) grated cheddar cheese and 1 Tbsp. (15 mL) chopped rosemary*

Quick Breakfast Bread Mix

AT BREAKFAST OR TEATIME, this quick bread base is delicious warm or cool with a touch of butter. Like the muffin mix recipe, use whatever you may have in the refrigerator to turn this loaf into your own special recipe.
Makes 1 loaf

1	egg	1
1¼ cups	milk	300 mL
1 tsp.	vanilla extract	5 mL
4 Tbsp.	vegetable oil	60 mL
2½ cups	all purpose flour	600 mL
1 cup	sugar	240 mL
1 Tbsp.	baking powder	15 mL
1 tsp.	salt	5 mL

Preheat oven to 350°F (175°C) and grease a loaf pan. Whisk together egg, milk, vanilla and oil. Combine dry ingredients and add the liquids to them. Blend just until batter becomes smooth.

Add desired fruit or flavoring and spoon into loaf pan.

Bake for 45 to 55 minutes, until a tester inserted into middle of loaf comes out clean. Allow to cool for 10 minutes before removing from loaf pan.

The flavor of a basic quick bread can be easily changed by adding any of the following:
- *1 cup (240 mL) pitted sour cherries and ½ tsp. (2.5 mL) almond extract*
- *1 cup (240 mL) blueberries, raspberries or cranberries with 1 tsp. (5 mL) lemon zest*
- *½ cup (120 mL) sliced peaches and ½ cup (120 mL) blackberries*
- *1 cup (240 mL) diced pear or apple and ¾ cup (180 mL) grated cheddar cheese*
- *½ cup (120 mL) brandy-soaked dried apricots and pitted prunes with ½ tsp. (2.5 mL) nutmeg*
- *1 Tbsp. (15 mL) lemon or orange zest with 2 Tbsp. (30 mL) poppyseeds*

Palmiers

THIS BREAKFAST OR TEATIME delight can be made from fresh sheets of puff pastry, but is most often made from scraps left from other preparations. Puff pastry scraps, once rolled, cannot be rolled again because the dough will not "puff" evenly. Palmiers are a great means to avoid waste and treat yourself at the same time. Once formed, palmiers can be frozen and baked when desired.

Makes 12 to 16 pieces

½ lb.	puff pastry dough (page 125)	225 g
⅓ cup	butter, melted	80 mL
½ cup	sugar	120 mL
½ tsp.	ground cinnamon	2.5 mL

Preheat oven to 400°F (200°C). On a lightly floured surface, roll out puff pastry to ¼-inch-thick (.6-cm) rectangle. Brush pastry with melted butter. Combine sugar and cinnamon and sprinkle ¼ cup (60 mL) on pastry. Starting at one short end, roll pastry until you reach the middle of the sheet. From the other side, repeat until the 2 rolls are touching. Brush meeting point with butter and sprinkle with 1 Tbsp. (15 mL) sugar.

Slice into pieces 1 inch (2.5 cm) wide. Dip bottom of each slice into melted butter and then into remaining cinnamon sugar and place, sugared side down, on a greased or parchment-lined baking sheet.

Bake for 15 to 20 minutes, until rich golden brown and crispy.

169

"Palmiers" is a nice name, and sounds almost exotic. We had an exchange student from Germany who was working with us who, when asked to make these, looked puzzled. When shown, she exclaimed, "Oh, you mean Pigs' Ears!" Try them yourself and you'll see.

Granola

GRANOLA SEEMS to be popular at the restaurant in any season and is tasty served with yogurt or milk. The scent as it is baking in the oven regularly draws the staff into the bakeshop out of curiosity (and hopes of a taste!)

Makes 6 cups (1.5 L)

2 cups	oats	475 mL
1/2 cup	wheat bran	120 mL
1/2 cup	sesame seeds	120 mL
1/2 cup	coconut (optional)	120 mL
1/2 cup	hazelnuts, chopped	120 mL
1/2 cup	sunflower seeds	120 mL
1/2 cup	vegetable oil	120 mL
1/2 cup	honey	120 mL
1 tsp.	cinnamon	5 mL
dash	salt	dash
dash	vanilla extract	dash
1/2 cup	chopped dried apricots	120 mL
1/2 cup	dried cherries	120 mL
1/2 cup	raisins	120 mL
	zest of 1 lemon or 1 orange	

Preheat oven to 325°F (165°C). In a bowl, combine oats, bran, sesame, coconut, hazelnuts and sunflower seeds.

Heat oil, honey, cinnamon, salt and vanilla in a small pot until honey is softened and mixture is blended. Pour over oats and stir well. Spread onto a greased or parchment-lined baking sheet and bake for 20 to 30 minutes, stirring occasionally, until rich golden brown in color. Remove from oven and add fruits and zest. Allow to cool before breaking into pieces.

This recipe has been one of our most commonly requested. It stores well in the pantry in airtight containers.

Lemon Cornmeal Pancakes
with Citrus Syrup

LIGHT IN TEXTURE and flavor, a mix of orange and grapefruit replaces the traditional maple syrup accompaniment.

Be careful not to overmix pancake batter. This develops the glutens in the flour and produces a chewy, as opposed to a fluffy, pancake. A few lumps in the batter are just fine – they will work themselves out.

Serves 4

2 cups	all purpose flour	475 mL
¼ cup	cornmeal	60 mL
2 Tbsp.	sugar	30 mL
2 Tbsp.	baking powder	30 mL
1 tsp.	salt	5 mL
2 cups	milk	475 mL
2	eggs	2
¼ cup	vegetable oil	60 mL
	zest of 1 lemon	

Citrus Syrup

2	red grapefruits	2
3	oranges	3
3 Tbsp.	honey	45 mL
dash	vanilla extract	dash

Combine flour, cornmeal, sugar, baking powder and salt. Mix in milk, eggs, vegetable oil and zest until just mixed. Heat a skillet over medium heat and grease lightly. Ladle batter in desired shape and size and cook until top surface loses its shine. Turn and cook until golden brown. Pancakes can be kept warm by covering and holding in a low-temperature oven.

To prepare glaze, section grapefruits and oranges, removing outside skin and reserving liquid. Place segments and juice in a small saucepot with honey and vanilla over low heat, just to warm and melt honey. Spoon over pancakes.

At the restaurant, we serve these pancakes with lavender butter, a mixture of finely chopped lavender leaves with softened unsalted butter. As the butter melts over the pancakes, the summery scent of lavender is emitted, and tastes wonderful with the honeyed citrus syrup.

Brioche French Toast
with Balsamic Glazed Cherries

WHAT BETTER MEDIUM is there for any egg batter than egg and butter bread? Leftover brioche absorbs batter without getting soggy, and cooks up into a decadently rich breakfast treat. The cherries reduced with balsamic vinegar complement the toast, as the acidity in the cherries offsets its richness.

Serves 4

4	eggs	4
⅔ cup	milk	160 mL
dash	nutmeg	dash
8–12	slices Brioche (page 161)	8–12
1 cup	Balsamic Glazed Cherries (page 178)	240 mL

Whisk together eggs, milk and nutmeg. Heat a skillet over medium heat and grease lightly. Dip brioche slices, a couple at a time, in egg mixture and place in skillet. Brown evenly on both sides.

Heat Balsamic Glazed Cherries and spoon over French toast.

 Spreading butter on this recipe of French toast is not really necessary because of the butter already built into the bread. Try instead a dollop of crème fraîche with a touch of brown sugar stirred into it.

172

Western Omelette Crepes

THIS DIGNIFIED COUSIN to the toasted western sandwich is great to serve for brunch, whether cooking for 2 or 12.

Serves 4

1	recipe Crepe Batter (page 126)	1
4	green onions, chopped	4
8	eggs	8
1/2 cup	milk	120 mL
	salt and pepper	
dash	ground nutmeg	dash
1 Tbsp.	unsalted butter or vegetable oil	15 mL
1	red bell pepper, diced	1
1/2 cup	ham, diced	120 mL
1 tsp.	fresh thyme or basil, chopped	5 mL
1 cup	cheddar cheese, grated	240 mL

Add 2 of the chopped green onions to the crepe batter and mix well. Prepare crepes as instructed in the basic crepe recipe. After making, keep crepes warm by covering and placing them in a low-temperature oven.

Whisk together eggs, milk, salt and pepper and nutmeg until evenly blended. Heat a pan over medium heat and sauté peppers in butter or oil until tender, about 2 minutes. Add remaining green onions, ham and herbs and sauté 2 minutes more. Reduce heat to low and add egg mixture. With a wooden spoon, slowly stir eggs until almost cooked. Add cheddar cheese and stir until melted.

To serve, place 2 crepes on each plate. Fill one side with eggs and fold crepe over. Repeat with each crepe.

Instead of crepes, try this egg mixture with pasta for a quick lunch; I call it "Spaghetti Western."

Omelette with Chevalier Brie
and Peach and Pepper Relish

MASTERING THE ART of making omelettes just takes a little practice, and rarely are unsuccessful attempts so far gone as to be inedible. Chevalier Brie is a triple-cream cheese from Quebec that is similar to St. André. The peach and pepper relish adds a sweetness and a light acidity that work very well with eggs and cheese.

Serves 4

8	eggs	8
4 Tbsp.	milk or water	60 mL
	salt and pepper	
1 Tbsp.	vegetable oil or butter	15 mL
6 oz.	Chevalier Brie	170 g
$\frac{1}{2}$ cup	Peach and Pepper Relish (page 179)	120 mL

Whisk together eggs, milk or water and salt and pepper. Heat a small omelette pan or non-stick coated pan over medium-high heat. Add a touch of vegetable oil or butter and ladle in $\frac{1}{4}$ of the egg mixture. Immediately begin stirring eggs with a spatula, shaking the pan slightly at the same time.

Continue stirring until eggs start to pull away from the sides of the pan. This will only take 2 minutes. Place cheese on top of omelette and set aside for 2 minutes. This will set the bottom of the omelette without browning it, and allow the cheese to melt.

To turn out onto plate, flip $\frac{1}{3}$ of omelette over itself, covering the cheese. Lift the pan over the plate, and let the omelette fall over itself and onto the plate. Spoon peach and pepper relish over omelette and serve.

Note: If you have more than one omelette pan, you can make one and let it set while beginning the second one. When the cook is well-practiced, 4 people should be eating their omelettes in a matter of minutes. If this is asking the impossible, just keep omelettes warm in a low-temperature oven until all are ready.

An omelette is one of the few egg dishes that is cooked over high heat. A well-made omelette is not browned on the outside. A trick we use at the restaurant is to place the omelette pan in a 350°F (175°C) oven for 30 to 45 seconds after the cheese has been placed on it. This soufflés the eggs a little, without overcooking them, to produce a very fluffy result.

174

Honey-Mustard Glazed Sausage

WE USE A GOOD-QUALITY honey-garlic sauage for breakfast at the restaurant, not the overly fatty sage breakfast sausage. An alternative to bacon, this is a great way to use leftover sausage from the barbeque the night before. The honey caramelizes onto the sausage, creating a delectable treat that is tasty with your eggs, pancakes or French toast.

Serves 4

³/₄ lb.	honey-garlic sausage	340 g
1¹/₂ Tbsp.	coarse-grain mustard	22.5 mL
2 Tbsp.	honey	30 mL

In a sauté pan over medium heat, cook sausages through (or reheat leftover sausages in a touch of oil). Coat sausages evenly with mustard and honey and cook until honey caramelizes onto sausages.

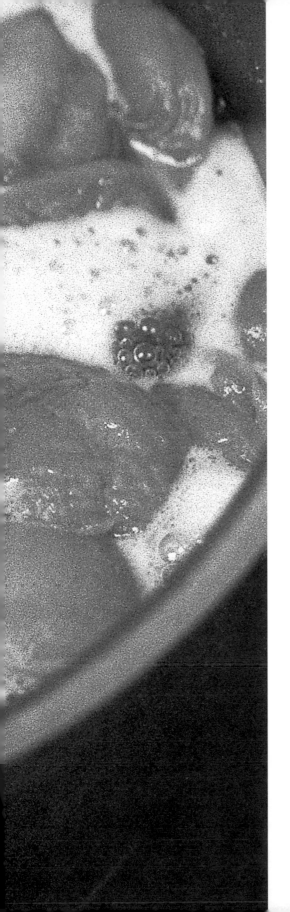

RELISHES AND PRESERVES

Putting down fruits, tomatoes or vegetables is like making a wise, short-term investment.

In the past, preserving was done during harvest in order to survive the winter, whereas we currently see it as a way of capturing excess produce at its peak, or celebrating family traditions.

Opening a jar of relish in the cold winter months seems to let rays of sunshine into the kitchen. I remember a great New Year's brunch with Omelettes with Chevalier Brie and Peach and Pepper Relish. We were moving forward with a reminder of something good from the past.

Consult a home canning book if you are unfamiliar with procedure. Spend a day with your family and start your own tradition. We prepare many of these preserves as take-home gifts for guests; why not make some to pass on to your friends?

Maple Gamay Rhubarb Compote

SERVED WARM, this compote is a delicious taste of spring atop vanilla ice cream. As well, rhubarb compote has savory applications as a sauce for trout, chicken or pork. The Gamay wine adds to the pink color of fresh rhubarb in season.

Yields 8 cups (2 L)

12 cups	diced rhubarb	3 L
	juice of 3 lemons	
2 cups	Gamay wine	475 mL
4 cups	sugar	950 mL
1 cup	pure maple syrup	240 mL
1 tsp.	salt	5 mL

Place all ingredients in a non-reactive pot and simmer, stirring occasionally, until rhubarb is soft and fully cooked but still retains its shape, about 45 minutes.

Compote can be frozen or jarred.

If the rhubarb stalks are thick, the outside may be tough. This can be rectified by peeling the rhubarb. Simply take a paring knife and cut a small section off the outside of the stalk. Pull down and away from the stalk and the outside membrane will easily peel away.

Balsamic Glazed Cherries

THIS PRESERVE should be made when sour cherries are in peak season.

The delicious flavor of cherries with balsamic vinegar complements savory dishes such as chicken, duck or cold roast pork, but also pairs well with sweets like chocolate and ice cream.

Yields 4 cups (950 mL)

3 lbs.	sour cherries, pitted	1.35 kg
1 lb.	sugar	455 g
1 cup	balsamic vinegar	240 mL

Place all ingredients in a large pot and simmer until sugar, vinegar and cherry juices have reduced to a glaze (when the sauce coats the back of a spoon). This usually takes 1 to $1\frac{1}{2}$ hours.

Cherries can be frozen or jarred.

Sour cherries tend to lose their color halfway through cooking this compote, but it does return as the liquid reduces. Don't worry if the cherries look a little orange and deflated; it all works out in the end.

Gooseberry Relish

WITH LUNCHMEAT, pork or meat pies, this relish adds a distinctive flavor. Both the green, tart berries and the riper pink berries can be used in this recipe.

Yields 8 cups (2 L)

2	large white onions, julienned	2
6 cups	gooseberries, stems removed	1.5 L
1 cup	white vinegar	240 mL
2 cups	sugar	475 mL
1½ Tbsp.	whole mustard seed	22.5 mL
1 tsp.	salt	5 mL

Place all ingredients in a large pot and simmer until onions are tender and half the gooseberries have split. Sugar may have to be adjusted, depending on the sweetness of the gooseberries.

Relish can be frozen or jarred.

Any preparation using vinegar should be cooked in a stainlees steel or other non-reactive pot. Aluminum pots react with the acidity and add a metallic taste to the prepared foods. Also, use wooden or heat-proof plastic utensils to stir relishes to avoid any reaction.

Peach and Pepper Relish

THIS COLORFUL RELISH is delicious with cheese, eggs, chicken or fish. Firm peaches are best, as they hold their shape when cooked.

Yields 12 cups (3 L)

12	peaches, peeled and diced	12
12	red bell peppers, diced	12
⅔ cup	white vinegar	160 mL
1	lemon, halved	1
1	jalapeño pepper, optional	1
3 cups	sugar	720 mL

Place peaches, peppers, vinegar, lemon and jalapeño pepper, if using, into a non-reactive (stainless steel) pot and bring to a simmer. Simmer for 30 minutes, stirring occasionally.

Add sugar and simmer 30 minutes more. Remove lemon and jalapeño pepper. Relish can be frozen or jarred.

One day, a server brought in a sample of this relish that his mother, Ginnie Douglas, had prepared. Little did she know that we would end up putting it on the menu and featuring it, always with favorable response. Thanks, Ginnie!

Pickled Green Tomatoes

WHEN THINNING your tomato plants, there is no need to discard the little green runts, pickle 'em! Delicious in the place of cucumber pickles, green tomatoes offer an appeal to the eye as well as the palate.
Yields 6 cups (1.5 L)

6 cups	green tomatoes, quartered	1.5 mL
2 Tbsp.	whole mustard seed	30 mL
2	bay leaves	2
1 Tbsp.	black peppercorns	15 mL
3	cloves garlic, peeled	3
1	onion, julienned	1
4 cups	white vinegar	950 mL

To jar tomatoes, toss tomatoes with spices, garlic and onion and evenly distribute into jars. Heat vinegar to boiling (be careful not to inhale) and pour it over tomatoes. Following proper canning procedures, seal jars immediately.

If storing tomatoes in the refrigerator, allow to cool, then chill. Tomatoes will keep 6 to 8 weeks refrigerated.

> *Once a faint "star" appears on the smooth end of a tomato, it will start to ripen. Store your tomatoes in a cool dark place and allow them to soften and develop sweetness.*

Pickled Beets

ONE OF OUR MOST popular salads at Inn on the Twenty is a composition of pickled beets with roasted pear and goat cheese.
Yields 6 cups (1.5 L)

12	beets	12
1	onion, julienned	1
1 Tbsp.	black peppercorns	15 mL
4	whole cloves	4
1	orange	1
4 cups	white vinegar	1 L

Cook beets in water with a splash of vinegar until tender, 30 to 40 minutes. Drain and cool. Peel beets and cut into wedges. Place beets in jars with onion, peppercorns and cloves. Peel orange with a vegetable peeler and put skin into jars.

Heat vinegar to a boil and pour it over beets. Jar immediately, following proper canning procedure, or cool and refrigerate. Beets will keep 6 to 8 weeks refrigerated.

Hot Pickled Mushrooms

THIS IS ONE OCCASION where we call solely for the use of button mushrooms. The pickling process negates any flavor that a more exotic mushroom has. Pickled mushrooms are a tasty part of an antipasto plate.

Yields 4 cups (950 mL)

4 Tbsp.	olive oil	60 mL
3 lbs.	button mushrooms	1.35 kg
1 cup	balsamic vinegar	240 mL
1	clove garlic, minced	1
1 tsp.	fresh thyme, chopped	5 mL
1 tsp.	salt	5 mL

Heat a large skillet over medium-high heat until it begins to smoke. Add oil and mushrooms. Stir mushrooms regularly and cook until all liquid evaporates from the pan, about 15 minutes.

Add vinegar, garlic, thyme and salt and reduce heat to medium. Continue cooking and stirring until all vinegar has been absorbed. This takes 10 to 15 minutes.

Serve warm, or chilled the next day as a relish.

Mushrooms are mostly water, so the reducing involved in this recipe intensifies the natural flavors. The mushrooms initially fry, then release water and poach in their own juices. Allow the mushrooms to fry a second time after the liquid has evaporated before you add the vinegar, garlic and thyme.

Thyme-Infused Honey

FLAVORED HONEY is a great accent for an omelette and is fantastic with strong or rich cheeses, to soften the kick without masking the taste. Infused honey poured into a decorative bottle makes a great gift.

Yields 2 cups (475 mL)

2 cups	honey	475 mL
2	bunches fresh thyme	2

Place honey and thyme (stems and all) in a pot and heat over a low temperature. Allow flavor to infuse for 30 minutes.

Thyme can be strained off while honey is warm, or left in to infuse further.

Other herbs also taste wonderful. Sage and rosemary pair well with chicken and pork. Try buckwheat honey; its earthiness takes herb flavors easily.

KITCHEN TOOLS

Considering the amount of time we spend in our kitchens, it is important that they are comfortable, well lit and reasonably well equipped. Fancy kitchen tools may not make your food taste better, but they can make cooking a lot easier.

Hand Blender

Many people have these at home and never use them. They work effectively and are much easier to move around and clean than a full-size food processor. At home we have a model with variable speeds and a quick-release head for easy wash-up. To purée soups, just drop the blade end into the cooking pot and "buzz" until smooth—very simple indeed. Hand blenders also work for mayonnaise, milkshakes, vinaigrettes and fruit purées.

Instant-Read Thermometer

These come in analog or digital and provide accurate instant measurements that can be used for meats or sugar. Some have a probe that can be placed directly in the oven, and read the temperature as your holiday turkey roasts.

Japanese Mandolin

A mandolin is like a plane with an adjustable blade and comb for slicing or shredding vegetables. Traditional stainless steel models are quite expensive, but some Asian markets sell a plastic model that stays razor sharp for years.

Knives

Keep them sharp! Buy a steel and use it often by drawing the knife blade along either side of the steel several times at a 30-degree angle. If you're not handy, get your knives sharpened by a professional. A very expensive dull knife is still just a dull knife.

The knives listed below are the basics.

BREAD KNIFE: The serrated edge is best for slicing bread, cakes, pastry and ripe tomatoes.

COOK'S OR FRENCH KNIFE: This is the handiest kitchen tool. Choose one that fits comfortably in your hand; if you have small hands, you may not want a huge blade.

PARING KNIFE: Plastic handled ones work fine and, after being used as a screwdriver, paint scraper and leather punch, won't cost much to replace.

Outdoor Grill

Have you got gas? For many, the convenience and speed of propane or natural gas is the answer. Adding the stems of fresh thyme or rosemary to the fire gives off a tremendous natural smoke flavor (although the neighbors may wonder what you're "smoking"). It's handy to have a small side table near the grill to keep tools, salt, sauce and a cooler or ice bucket with the perishables (I mean chicken, not beer!).

At home, we have a battery of outdoor cooking equipment and I do like to use charcoal. If we are going to the trouble of the real BBQ experience, I feel that lighting and burning down the coals is just part of the ritual.

Scale

For baking, precise measurements are very important. In addition to measuring cups and spoons, a scale will come in handy to ensure that your recipe will turn out as intended.

Wood Rasp

The new darling of culinary trends, this woodworking tool works like a charm for zesting lemons, grating Parmesan cheese and mincing ginger or garlic.

GLOSSARY

We have included here terminology that we have used in our recipes.

Blindbake: To cook pastry under foil or parchment paper that is weighted with pie weights, uncooked rice or dry beans.
Braise: A combination of dry and moist heat cooking. Item is first seared in butter or oil, then slowly cooked in liquid, as in stew.
Brunoise: A very fine dice.

Caramelize: To concentrate the natural sugars in food through slow cooking. Food takes on a rich golden color when caramelized.
Chiffonade: To cut into "ribbons." It is a fine shred of lettuce or herbs.
Cream: To mix butter and sugar until it is a fluffy consistency.

Debeard: To pull the hair-like piece from mussels. It is not harmful to eat, but neither is it palatable.
Deglaze: To pour cold liquid, such as wine, into a hot pan to loosen the caramelized particles that are full of flavor.
Devein: To remove the intestinal tract from shrimp, by scoring the top of the shrimp with a paring knife and removing the black vein.

Dice: To cut into small cubes, $\frac{1}{2}$ inch (1.2 cm) wide.

Gluten: The sticky protein that gives strength and elasticity to dough. An allergy to gluten is referred to as "celiac."

Gratin: To cook in a shallow dish until rich golden brown. The term classic refers to browning with cheese on top.

Julienne: To cut into slender strips.

Mince: To chop very finely.

Parchment paper: Silicon, heat-proof paper used to prevent food from sticking to the pan.

Pinbones: The small bones found in some fish fillets, especially salmon and trout. These can be removed with a pair of tweezers.

Poach: To cook in liquid just below a simmer; an appropriate method for delicate foods such as fish or fruit.

Proof/Rise: To allow yeast to ferment and leaven dough.

Reduce: To cook slowly to evaporate water from a soup, stock or sauce. Used to concentrate flavor.

Refresh/Shock: To chill in ice water after cooking. Helps retain color and flavor.

Sear: To brown the surface of meat or fish over high heat to seal in natural juices.

Soft peak: To whip egg whites or cream to the point where they gently curl when the whisk or beater is lifted.

Zest: The outside skin of citrus fruit which contains flavorful oils, used in baking and marinating.

INDEX

185

191